Central Asia and India

Emerging Extended Neighbourhood

Central Asia and India

Emerging Extended Neighbourhood

Edited by

Kashif Hasan Khan
Director, Silk Road Research Centre,
Ala-Too International University, Bishkek, Kyrgyzstan

New Century Publications
New Delhi, India

NEW CENTURY PUBLICATIONS
4800 / 24, Bharat Ram Road,
Ansari Road, Daryaganj,
New Delhi - 110 002 (India)

Tel.: 011-2324 7798, 4358 7398, 4101 7798

E-mail: info@newcenturypublications.com

www.newcenturypublications.com

Editorial office:
4832/24, Ansari Road, Daryaganj,
New Delhi – 110 002

Tel.: 011-4356 0919

First Published: **2020**

ISBN: **978-81-7708-498-6**

Published by New Century Publications and printed at Milan Enterprises, New Delhi.

Designs: Patch Creative Unit, New Delhi.

PRINTED IN INDIA

Foreword

The energy reserves of Central Asia are unquestionably significant and can, to a certain extent, address India's growing demand for energy. However, geography, geopolitics, and security in India's neighbourhood are challenges that have to be overcome. A meaningful and co-operative relationship with Central Asian countries can be established by adopting an innovative approach coupled with high level of diplomatic exchanges. As mentioned in this book, despite many efforts there is still a need to do much more from both the sides.

There are some highly serious issues like connectivity and the growing influence of China in Central Asia. China's involvement in key infrastructure projects for larger strategic purposes like China-Pakistan Economic Corridor (CPEC) will lead to strengthened politico-economic relations. What does all this mean for India's outreach in the region?

The present book provides deep insights into various aspects of India-Central Asia relations. It contains research papers on the subject authored by scholars from different countries. The book will surely add to the existing body of literature on India-Central Asia relations and provide new information and analysis for young researchers, foreign policy practitioners and already established academicians.

I hope that many more researchers in India, Central Asia and elsewhere will focus their interest on the important issues raised in this book. I congratulate Dr. Kashif Hasan Khan for his efforts to bring out this valuable work. I wish him a great success!

Dr. Sanzharbek Erdolatov
Rector, Ala-Too International University
Bishkek, Kyrgyzstan

Acknowledgements

There are people to whom I am especially indebted and whose assistance was invaluable in completing this publication.

I place on record my deep sense of gratitude to the Rector of Ala-Too International University, Dr. Sanzharbek Erdolatov, and Vice Rector, Dr. Halil Koch for their immense support and encouragement throughout the progress of this project.

I am highly thankful to all the contributors to this work who hail from different countries and specialize in the study of India-Central Asia relations. Their thought-provoking ideas on the subject will provide immensely useful inputs to those who want to broaden their knowledge on India-Central Asia multi-faceted relations and challenges thereof.

I also express appreciation and gratitude to my beloved parents, my three lovely sisters and brother and my awesome wife, Saiba, for unfailing love and moral support for my academic pursuits. And worth to mention that by the time I finished this project, God gave a very cute son, Yaqub.

Thanks are also due to the anonymous editors of New Century Publications, New Delhi for their help and co-operation at various stages of the publication of this book.

Still, I take full responsibility for any kind of lapses in interpretations and analyses that might have crept into this work.

About the Book

Relations between India and Central Asian countries are centuries old. Despite having deep historical and cultural ties, the two regions have not been very successful in establishing strong economic and trade ties. This unsatisfactory performance is attributable to a host of factors, the chief being poor logistics, transportation difficulties, and geo-political situations.

Nevertheless, a good trade relationship with the Central Asian Republics is of high strategic importance for India. The countries of Central Asia have enormous amount of energy resources, which could help meet India's ever increasing energy requirements. These countries have a huge consumer market for a range of goods and services produced in India. Therefore, Central Asia holds a very significant position in India's foreign policy discourse. Obviously, India has made this region a significant part of its *extended neighbourhood policy*.

Central Asia region consists of five culturally and ethnically diverse countries that have followed different paths to political and economic transformation since achieving independence from the erstwhile Soviet Union. Kazakhstan and Kyrgyzstan have, in relative terms, made strides in market reforms while Turkmenistan and Uzbekistan have not yet completed their transitions to market economies. Tajikistan represents an intermediate case.

The present volume contains seven research articles authored by scholars specializing in the field of India-Central Asia relations. Their studies provide deep insights into various facets of these relations, adding immensely to the existing literature on the subject.

About the Editor

Dr. Kashif Hasan Khan is currently Director, Silk Road Research Centre, Ala-Too International University, Bishkek, Kyrgyzstan. He has previously worked in the corporate sector as an international business consultant. He has worked in Turkey, Philippines, England and India. His research and teaching interests include international business, international trade theories, and the economy of Central Asia and history of economic thoughts. Dr. Kashif has written a number of articles, and attended and coordinated national and international conferences in India and abroad. His major work has been with ADB (Asian Development Bank), Minorities Commission of India as well as the IT sector.

Contents

Contributors

Dr. Kashif Hasan Khan is Director, Silk Road Research Centre, Ala-Too International University, Bishkek, Kyrgyzstan. He has previously worked in the corporate sector as an International Business Consultant. He has worked in Turkey, Philippines, England and India. His research and teaching interests include international business, international trade theories, the economy of Central Asia and history of economic thoughts. Kashif has written a number of articles, and attended and coordinated national and international level conferences in India and abroad. His major work has been with ADB (Asian Development Bank), Minorities Commission of India as well as the IT sector.

Dr. Athar Zafar is a Research Fellow at Indian Council of World Affairs (ICWA), New Delhi. Prior to joining ICWA, he was working with British Broadcasting Corporation, New Delhi. The scholar has visited several countries, including Russia and Central Asian Republics. Apart from English, Hindi and Urdu, he also knows Tajiki.

Dr. Anirban Chatterjee is Assistant Professor at the Department of Political Science, Plassey College, University of Kalyani, West Bengal, India. He earned his Ph.D. titled "Russian Response towards Western Democracy Promotion in the Post-Soviet Space, 2003-2015" from the Centre for Russian and Central Asian Studies, School of International Studies, Jawaharlal Nehru University (JNU), New Delhi.

Mr. Edilbekuulu Syimyk is a Ph.D. scholar at the Diplomatic Academy of Ministry of Foreign Affairs of the Kyrgyz Republic, International University of Kyrgyzstan, Bishkek, Kyrgyzstan.

Dr. Meha Pant is an Assistant Professor at the Amity Institute of International Studies, Amity University, Noida. She earned her Ph.D. degree from Jawaharlal Nehru University (JNU), New

Delhi on the topic "Transnational Border Security Threats and State Capacity in Central Asia: A Case study of the State of Tajikistan". She has contributed a number of articles to this field.

Dr. Erkin Baydarov is Orientalist and Researcher at the R.B. Suleimenov Institute of Oriental Studies, Committee of Science MES RK, Almaty, Kazakhstan. He is a member of the editorial board of the International Journal of Philosophy and Life (Journal of Philosophy and Life, Uzbekistan).

Mr. Rahul Dev is Assistant Professor at Kurukshetra University, Haryana, India. He has done M.A. in Politics and International Studies from Jawaharlal Nehru University (JNU), New Delhi. He is presently pursuing his Ph.D. from the same University.

Mrs. Zhansaya Zhangabulova is a Ph.D. scholar at the Eurasian National University named after L.N. Gumilyov, Astana, Kazakhstan. She earned her Masters Degree from People's Friendship University of Russia, Moscow, Russia. She has published several articles in national and international journals, and attended several international conferences.

Introduction

Kashif Hasan Khan

This book is a compendium of papers from the international conference "India and Central Asia Relations: Economic, Historical and Cultural Perspective" held in Bishkek from April 26-27, 2019 in Bishkek, Kyrgyzstan. The editor of this book was the main organizer of the conference. The chapters are written by academics and researchers from India and Central Asia. The volume aims to provide a better understanding of India-Central Asia multi-faceted relations in rapidly evolving geo-strategic dynamics. It provides valuable and timely insights into the contours of states' policies, particularly what role India plays in its extended neighbourhood as regards the Central Asian Republics.

Energy is one of Central Asia's crucial resources and the region intends to accelerate and harness this potential as an integral part of its economic development. The development of energy sector is expected to usher in enormous economic benefits in the form of infrastructure development, industrialization and huge revenue. With an increase in hydrocarbons and generation of hydropower in Central Asia, the republics of the region aim to not only provide domestic energy at an affordable cost; but also turn into net energy exporters in the near future which would have an impact on global energy demand (Wani, 2014).

However, because of Central Asia's political and economic instability, nations have transformed their policies from time to time in order to reap benefits from the region. The literature available in the field of historical, cultural, economic, political, strategic and security relations between India-CARs (Central Asian Republics) indicate that despite extensive literature on the subject, it falls short in highlighting the reasons for the development of the India-CARs relationship in the post-Cold war period (especially after 1991) and the convergence of economic interests and the various constraints within the mutual relationship. In some of the available literature, one or two aspects of the relationship are touched upon but all the issues which hamper or facilitate India-Central Asia relations are not dealt with in any of the available literature. Therefore, this work is an endeavour to fill these gaps in the literature and seeks to analyze various reasons for the development of bilateral relationship and challenges between India and the CARs in the post-Cold war era.

Throughout the 19th and 20th centuries, Central Asia was the scene of intense geopolitical struggle and the Great Game [1] between the British and Russian Empires, and later between the Soviet Union and the West, over Afghanistan and neighbouring territories. In the 21st century, Central Asia has become an area of renewed geopolitical interest, dubbed as the New Great Game [2] and is largely based on the region's hydrocarbon and mineral wealth. On top of that, the region is now perhaps the most important node in the implementation of China's Belt and Road Initiative (BRI) through which Beijing aims to get direct access to the Western markets. Moreover, since the Central Asian states are weak in the production of consumer goods, decision about establishing the regional Shanghai Cooperation Organization (SCO) is considered to be a major initiative taken by China to forward its security and economic interests in the region (The Times of Central Asia, 2019).

The relationship between India and Central Asia is centuries old. 1991 was a very decisive year for both the regions. India opened up its economy by bringing up liberalization policy which helped India to access and integrate with the world economy. And the CARs had just been declared as more dependent economies and it was high time to have more autonomy as earlier international trade had been planned and executed in Moscow. Despite having deep historical and cultural ties, the two regions have not been very successful in gaining great economic and trade ties.

There are many challenges that led to the trade gap between

the two. The top challenges include logistics, transportation difficulties, and geopolitical situations. Keeping these in view, a revival of the ancient 'silk-road' is the other notion that looms large time to time for enhancing the economic linkages to this region.

Nevertheless, a good trade relationship with the Central Asian Republics is of high strategic importance for India, since these countries are sandwiched between major powers like Russia, China, and Europe, and have an enormous amount of energy resources, which could help meet India's energy requirements and sustain its high economic growth (Agrawal, P., 2013). India and Central Asia complement each other in considerable manpower and markets. CARs have a huge consumer market for a range of goods and services. India has huge potential to be a reliable partner. Therefore, Central Asia holds a very significant position in India's foreign-policy discourse, as India has made the region a part of its "extended neighbourhood". In view of gaining strategic importance on account of trade, there is an enormous scope for pragmatic and profitable cooperation with India.

The Central Asian Republics consist of five culturally and ethnically diverse countries that have followed different paths to political and economic transformation in the past 25 years since achieving independence from the Soviet Union. Kazakhstan and Kyrgyzstan have in relative terms made strides in market reforms, while Turkmenistan and Uzbekistan have not yet completed their transitions to market economies. Tajikistan represents an intermediate case.

After experiencing more than a decade of growth based on hydrocarbon booms, the CAR countries are faced with increasing challenges resulting from falling commodity prices, declining trade and lower migrant remittances. The main policy challenge is to move away from commodity-based growth strategies to market-oriented diversification and adoption of broad spectrum of economic, institutional and political reforms. The major obstacles to political reforms and structural diversification in the five

Central Asian economies are internal and external geopolitical factors and deeply embedded institutional weaknesses within each country, particularly in areas where economic management interacts with authoritarian political systems and imperfect legal institutions (Batsaikan Uuriintiya, Dabrowski, 2017).

It is a good occasion to examine where they stand now, the results of their transitions from centrally planned to market economies and the challenges the region faces. Central Asia also makes an interesting study because of its landlocked location and its historic legacy, including seven decades of communist rule and central planning. Moreover, Central Asia remains relatively understudied compared to other regions. Despite their shared history and being referred to as a single region, the countries differ in their levels of political and economic development, cultural and ethnic composition and relations with the outside world.

In the1990s, Central Asia experienced many of the same hardships of economic transition as Central and Eastern European and other formerly communist countries, such as skyrocketing inflation, partial deindustrialization and the collapse of Soviet-type welfare systems. Turkmenistan and Uzbekistan have still not completed their transitions to market economies. Kazakhstan and Turkmenistan have joined the upper middle-income group, while Kyrgyzstan, Tajikistan and Uzbekistan remain in the lower-middle income category.

The countries of Central Asia are landlocked, although Kazakhstan and Turkmenistan border the Caspian Sea, which is not an open sea. Furthermore, the Soviet transportation network was concentrated on Russia and other Soviet republics, while connections with the outside world were almost non-existent. Despite some infrastructure investment in the last quarter of the century, the lack of connectivity between Central Asia and the outside world remains a major obstacle to trade and economic development. This is also true of intra-regional trade relations, which are impaired by the incompatibility of individual economic regimes, continuous political tensions, prolonged conflicts in the neighbourhood (Afghanistan) and partly closed borders.

In this background, there is a need to take another look at the various dimensions of the CARs relations with its neighbours and India in particular (Batsaikan Uuriintiya, Dabrowski, 2017). Therefore, in this book, an attempt has been made to analyze the socio-economic and political developments in Central Asia and the policy challenges faced by the region. In doing so, there is an examination of the historical background of the Central Asian transition, geography and geopolitics, trade and economic integration progress in economic reforms after 1991 and supporting role of external actors and socio-economic performance of the region.

After the collapse of the Soviet Union, the CARs not only needed capital investment, but they also needed sort of international recognition/attention. 9/11 was a game changer for the region because US interest in the region increased dramatically. The US paid the infant states more attention, and the assistance skyrocketed. Russia also tried to be more present in Central Asia to prevent excess American influence in the region, and China's interest in the region was also attaining more and more access. Resultantly, Central Asia suddenly found out that everyone needed them and they quickly adapted themselves to profit from these interests. They like competition in the region because they can benefit from countries competing over Central Asia. They are certainly not afraid of competition; it suits them just fine.

However, in the early 1990s, India's Central Asia policy was focused on Afghanistan. Over the years, India views Central Asia as a region that may contain terrorism from Afghanistan and Pakistan, while China is overwhelming the region with its economic growth. India's approach to regional organizations in Central Asia has been lukewarm, while China has taken the lead by forming and sustaining the Shanghai Cooperation Organization (SCO) (Patnaik, A., 2010). However, over the last decade, India has changed its outlook towards Central Asia. It perceives Central Asia as a buffer zone for developing economics and security. It has sought to expand counter terrorism cooperation and improve access to energy sources.

So far, India's relations in the region are affirmative, and fairly unsophisticated, as there are no major clashes between India and any of the Central Asian Republics. Historically, India's relations with CARs have also been close. Prior to 1990, India's warm relationship with the Soviet Union laid the foundation for amicable ties, and Pakistan's support for fundamentalist movements in the region served to push the countries even closer to India. Many believe that the relations between the two regions are friendly because of two reasons. Firstly, India does not share direct borders with any of the CARs that may lead to any dispute between the regions. Secondly, India's rivalry with Pakistan. Since Narendra Modi became the Prime Minister of India in 2014, the situation in Pakistan has been more tense as Modi leaves no effort to raise the issues of terrorism on public platforms.

India, Russia, and Iran signed an agreement in 2002, to establish the International North-South Transport Corridor (INSTC). This is a 7,200 km. transport network, which is vital to increase trade connectivity between India, Iran, Russia, CARs and Europe via network of roads, sea routes and rail. The initiative is an attempt to counter the Chinese One-Belt-One-Road (OBOR) initiative, which has the ability to connect China with over 60 states in Asia, Africa and Europe via a vast network of sea routes, road and rail. The INSTC will not only address the logistical issues between the two strategic partners, but will also reduce transportation cost and time. It is estimated that the Corridor will reduce the distance by 40 percent and the transportation cost by 30 percent.

In recent times, India's conciliatory and monetary quality has constrained it to expand its commitment beyond its immediate neighbourhood in South Asia to its 'broadened neighbourhood' in South East Asia, Persian Gulf, Central Asia and Caucuses; to guarantee its key financial, security and vitality interests. Over the last two decades, New Delhi has effectively sought after its 'Look

East Strategy', which is currently known as the 'Demonstration East Policy', while developing broad monetary and vital relations with its all-inclusive neighbours in South East Asia, to counter the Chinese impact.

The focus on its "extended neighbourhood" came into limelight when New Delhi announced its 'Connect Central Asia Policy' (CCAP) in 2012. Former Indian Prime Minister, Mr. P. V. Narasimha Rao, developed the "Look East" policy. Mr. Inder Kumar Gujral took it further by talking about India's "extended neighbourhood" encompassing the Persian Gulf, Central Asia and South East Asia. The External Affairs Minister, Mr. Jaswant Singh, emphasized the importance of engaging these regions more purposefully than it had previously. With trade becoming an important element of national strategy, the extended neighbourhood has begun to register in India's strategic consciousness.

But how does India translate the slogan of extended neighbourhood into concrete action? That is where the two new proposals on trans-regional cooperation come in. The first is about binding India and the Persian Gulf in a long-term energy relationship through a gas pipeline. It came up when Mr. Jaswant Singh travelled to Iran. Iran has abundant reserves of natural gas and wants to export it to India, whose thirst for hydrocarbon resources is enormous. Other countries on the Arab side of the Gulf such as Qatar and the Central Asian states such as Turkmenistan also have huge surpluses of natural gas. They would like to pump their natural gas into a pipeline to India, which has emerged as one of the top importers of petro products in the world (The Hindu, 2000).

This book is a collection of scholarly work and academic cooperation among researchers from various institutions. Consequently, it will help the readers/policymakers to have in-depth analysis of the region from different perspectives and its growing significance in contemporary international relations. The volume is a unique contribution to the literature on Central Asia as it focuses on emerging dimensions, and multiple regional implications of India-Central Asia interactions.

Athar Zafar in his paper, *Multilateral Engagements and India's Ties with Central Asia* acknowledges that in order to deepen the relations with the wider world, Central Asian countries adopted 'multi-vector' foreign policy in pursuance to their national interests. Though the Republics in the region adopted different growth paths suitable to their interest and requirements, India has maintained good relations with all the five, which paves the way to strengthening the multi-faceted inter-connectivity initiatives.

In his paper, *India-Tajikistan Relations: Vistas for Increasing Engagement*, Anirban Chatterjee discusses that the relations between Tajikistan and India are age old and historical. For India, Tajikistan's critical geo-strategic location of being situated in its 'extended neighbourhood' is important to accomplish its multifaceted interests. This has already been articulated through the 'Connect Central Asia' policy.

Edilbekuulu Syimyk's contribution on *Humanitarian Co-operation of India in Central Asia in the Context of Soft Power* considers the concept of soft power through the prism of modern geo-political and global processes. In its foreign policy strategy, India adheres to the principle of non-violence, while possessing exceptionally rich cultural and civilizational values. The article describes the influence of India on Central Asia, taking into account projects in the social and humanitarian fields. In conclusion, attempts are made to identify the main interests of India in Central Asia.

Meha Pant in her paper titled *Varied Paradigms, Co-ordination and Co-operation between the Two Regions* points out that the regions of Central Asia and India share a historical relationship which incorporates political, economic and cultural dimensions in a defined proportion. With a thaw in the relations amongst them during the Soviet rule and a later realization of the significance of Central Asia to India, all seems to have been working in the right direction for the two regions. Although, the regions seem to be cooperating with each other well on the economic front with the recent unveiling of the TAPI gas pipeline, yet there remain some dimensions which, though common, still remain unexplored to a large extent.

In his paper titled *India and Central Asian Countries: Moving Towards Each Other*, Erkin Baydarov argues that resource-rich Central Asia, through which passes a significant part of the infrastructure of the Belt and Road Initiative, attracts not only China, but also India. After gaining membership of the Shanghai Cooperation Organization (SCO), India is interested in expanding cooperation with Central Asian countries, as well as opening new opportunities in this direction.

Rahul Dev's paper *India-Central Asia Relations and the Stability of Afghanistan Post-2014* focuses on Central Asia, which is considered India's extended neighbourhood and has strong historical, cultural and economic relations with India since the time of the Silk Route. But the partition of India in 1947 and disintegration of the USSR in 1991 resulted in drifting away of these five Central Asian republics from India. This paper tries to analyze how both India and the CAR are important to each other, what role the recently concluded first ever India-Central Asia summit in Uzbekistan can play in that and how future cooperation may be enhanced.

In her paper, *Building Relations between India and Central Asia*, Zhansaya Zhangabulova refers to India's foreign policy in Central Asia which has passed through the stages of formation, institutionalization and some transformation due to external and internal factors. The revitalization of India's policies in the area is determined by the specific proximity to Afghanistan and the presence of possible security threats, such as illegal drug trafficking, terrorism and religious extremism, which may spread in the region. The Indian establishment is also pushing for the pursuit of a more intensive policy in Central Asia by fears related to the steady rise of China's financial, military and political weight. In addition to bilateral opportunities for cooperation, India may utilize some useful mechanisms to increase its influence in the Central Asian region.

Endnotes

1. The 'Great Game' is the term applied to the long-term contest between the British and Russians for influence in Central Asia, and particularly Afghanistan, during the 19th and early 20th centuries. The game was between Tsar Empire of Russia and Britain which was controlling India. There was always a fear in the British mind that Russia was a threat to the British colonies and the Tsarist Empire had to stop somewhere, and best place to stop was Afghanistan and Central Asia. Because of the said fear the British always wanted to control the foreign policy of Afghanistan. British used Afghanistan as a buffer state between the Tsarist Empire and the British Empire.
2. Central Asia has emerged geo-strategically as significant actor in the 'new Great Game', engaging Russia, China and the United States, all vying over their security and energy related interests in the region.

References

Agrawal, Pradeep and Seema Sangita (2013), "India and Central Asia: Trade Routes and Trade Potential", IEG Working Paper No. 334.

Nasr, Najeebullah (2018), "EAEU: India's Extended Neighbourhood in West", Centre for Strategic and Contemporary Research, available at: https://cscr.pk/explore/themes/trade-economics/eaeu-indias-extended-neighbourhood-west.

Pandey, Sanjay Kumar (2012), "India and the Importance of Central Asia", in Dash, P.L. (ed.), 'India and Central Asia: Two Decades of Transition', New Delhi: Oxford University Press.

Patnaik Ajay (2010), "Comparing India's and China's Approaches in Central Asia", OSCE: Central Asia Security Policy Brief, available at: http://www.osceacademy.net/upload/file/Ajay_Patnaik.pdf.

The Times of Central Asia, available at: https://www.timesca.com/index.php/news/21431-weekly-digest-of-central-asia-135.

Uuriintuya, Batsaikhan and Marek Dabrowski (2017), "Central Asia: Twenty-five Years after the Break-up of the USSR", *Russian Journal of Economics*, (3), pp. 296-320.

Abbreviations/Acronyms

ADB	Asian Development Bank
BRI	Belt and Road Initiative
CARs	Central Asian Republics
CIS	Commonwealth of Independent States
EBRD	European Bank for Reconstruction and Development
EEU	Eurasian Economic Union
FFFAI	Federation of Freight Forwarder's Association in India
FTA	Free Trade Agreement
GDP	Gross Domestic Product
ICCR	Indian Council for Cultural Relations
IMU	Islamic Movement of Uzbekistan
INSTC	International North-South Transport Corridor
ISI	Inter Service Intelligence
IT	Information Technology
ITEC	Indian Technical and Economic Cooperation
KTZ	Kazakhstan Temir Zholy
NATO	North Atlantic Treaty Organization
NSTC	North South Transport Corridor
OBOR	One Belt One Road
OIC	Organization of Islamic Cooperation
OSCE	Organization for Security and Cooperation in Europe
PoK	Pakistan Occupied Kashmir
PPP	Purchasing Power Parity
SCO	Shanghai Corporation Organization
SFK	Soros Foundation-Kyrgyzstan
TAPI	Turkmenistan-Afghanistan-Pakistan-India
UN	United Nations
UNGA	United Nation General Assembly
USSR	Union of Soviet Socialist Republics
WTO	World Trade Organization

1

Multilateral Engagements and India's Ties with Central Asia

Athar Zafar

India and the Central Asian region in its north enjoy deep historical connections, close cultural affinity, longstanding economic linkages and friendly people-to-people relations. In the past, parts of Indian subcontinent and areas of Central Asia have also been under single political authority. About 2000 years ago, the two regions, particularly India's northern parts had close interactions, particularly under the Kushana rulers (Thapar, 2000). Though presently, there have been no direct and unhindered land linkages between the subcontinent and Central Asia on account of changes in political geography resulting from partition of the subcontinent couple of decades ago, the people of the two regions always felt connected to each other, especially due to their deep civilizational connections. The world has witnessed that the interactions between India and the region have been productive and enriching to each other and contributed to the constructive global developments.

The interaction continued and sustained throughout the famed Cotton Route (Thakur, 2015), Silk Route and Spice Route (Mukherjee, 2014) days. These varied land and sea routes and their branches not only carried merchandize from different places to their destinations, but also assisted the flow and intermingling of ideas and values. The land paths also facilitated travel of learned people from various parts of the world to exchange and enrich wisdom, experience, knowledge and skills. Central Asia worked as a bridge for the travellers seeking to explore the then advanced civilization in South Asia. In fact, it can be said that hardly any two regions have such a close cultural connection as Central Asia has with the Indian subcontinent. The connection has been intense and varied. It is evident even today. People from the subcontinent visiting the region or the Central Asian people coming to India find themselves easy to engage with each other. They find many commonalities in their thinking, worldview or in the expression of art and architecture.

It is known that Buddhism has its initial progress in India. The rise of Buddhism, considered a revolutionary (Moon and Narake, 2014, p. 149) idea of the time, gradually found its acceptability in the Central Asian region and was welcomed by the people there. It is evident from various sites located across the vast territory of the region. One of the world's largest reclining Buddha sculptures was found in Tajikistan. The geographical location of Central Asia further helped Buddhism to spread in other directions.

No interaction, especially cultural, remains unidirectional. If the idea of Buddhism was received in Central Asia, a spiritual return from the region came in the form of Sufism. Some Sufi orders or the *Silsilahs*, which are popular in parts of India, including *Kubrawi* and *Naqshabandi*, have their beginnings in Central Asia. Among the earliest and prominent books on Sufism is *Kashful-ul-Mahjoob* and it was written in Indian subcontinent by Ali Hujwairi, who is popularly known as Hazrat Data Ganjbakhsh (Zafar and Anas, 2016). In his address at Nazarbayev University, Astana, Kazakhstan, in July 2015, Prime Minister Narendra Modi said: "The confluence of Indian and Islamic civilization took place in Central Asia. We enriched each other not only in spiritual thought, but also in medicine, science, mathematics and astronomy" (MEA, 2015). He added that the Islamic heritage of both India and Central Asia have been founded on the principle of love and devotion. It has always rejected the forces of extremism, he observed.

Similarly, language also binds the people of the subcontinent and Central Asia in common threads of expression and understanding. There are similarities, including in words and expressions, between *Rig Veda* and *Avesta*. Alberuni's works on India and *Tuzuk-e Babari* by Zahiruddin Babar are important sources of knowledge in the medieval period. Both these men hailed from regions of the present day Uzbekistan. Further, the linguistic synthesis achieved during the medieval period led in India, the development of a new genre in Persian/Tajik literature. It is known as *Sabk-e-Hindi* or the Indian School, the other two being *Sabk-e-Iraqi* and *Sabk-e Khorasani*.

India-Central Asia Relations

The shift of economic arteries of trade between East and West from land to waters in 15th-16th centuries onwards due to internal and external factors and subsequent emergence of naval powers in the Western world created adverse conditions contributing to the decline in economic and other engagements between Indian and Central Asian lands. Later, the interchanges were further restricted by the arrival of two different and competing colonial powers in Central Asia and in the subcontinent. Tsarist Russia moved from north to south and met the British Empire in Afghanistan/Central Asia, which was moving from south to north direction in the subcontinent in the 19th Century.

The empires created demarcations in the areas separating people and communities, who were interacting since times immemorial. Their manoeuvres in the converging zones of South Asia and Central Asia were primarily driven by the desire to serve the interests of empires that overlooked the aspirations of the people on the two sides of the divide. Their legacy lives on in the form of instability and absence of peace in certain areas even today. Following the Independence in 1947, India maintained relations with Central Asia in the Soviet times through visits and student exchanges. The end of Cold War and emergence of five republics in Central Asia is an opportunity for the two to rewrite the course of development in the region and create strong base for mutual development.

The end of the Union of Soviet Socialist Republic (USSR)

and emergence of five independent states of Kazakhstan, Kyrgyz Republic, Tajikistan, Turkmenistan and Uzbekistan in Central Asia in early 1990s was an unexpected development for India. The country had close political and economic relations with the USSR and it was also among the few countries given access to Central Asia. Even before the emergence of the region in the form of five independent republics, India's diplomatic relations with the region during the Soviet period was maintained through the Consulate General at Tashkent (Embassy of India website). Republics of the region and other countries around Central Asia were apparently not prepared for the demise of the USSR and formed independent states in the region (Olcott, 1992). There were no large-scale protests or demands for independence from the USSR, especially in Central Asia.

The world and its international politics were undergoing major transformations at the end of the Cold War. The USSR was unravelling and it was withdrawing after an unsustainable military campaign in Afghanistan. India had close relations with the USSR and the country was a critical trade partner for New Delhi. In 1990, the Soviet Union was the top goods exports market for India (Arun, 2017). Suddenly, a big market became uncertain for India as the whole Soviet space was facing an economic meltdown. India, on the other hand, was also at the cusp of major economic reforms during the same timeframe. The political conditions within the country were also consuming a lot of energy and concentration of the central government in Delhi. The situation within the respective countries in Central Asia and India kept themselves largely to themselves and internally focused despite initial interests shown by the two sides to establish and enhance bilateral ties.

India's Multilateral Approach to Engage Central Asia

In the early years of the Republics' independence, India, perhaps, faced a dilemma with regard to the direction of its relationship with the new states in Central Asia. Seemingly, New Delhi was also unsure of the foreign policy directions and the development path to be adopted by the five newly independent countries of the region. Nevertheless, the situation did not last long. India was among the first countries to establish diplomatic relations with all the five republics. In fact, it was among the first few countries to have ambassadorial presence in the region in all the republics. The republics gradually stabilized and India also made substantial economic progress following the structural economic reforms, which allowed it to develop at a faster rate and become an economic opportunity not only at the regional but also at the global scale. A major policy initiative came in the form of 'Connect Central Asia' policy announced in 2012 in Kyrgyzstan (Ministry of External Affairs, 2012).

The five republics could now independently decide their own destiny. Kazakhstan adopted economic reforms as a priority, while Kyrgyz Republic gave preference to domestic political reforms. Kyrgyzstan is the only republic in the region to initiate the parliamentary form of democracy. The country's constitution restricts Presidents to a single six-year term in office (BBC, 2017). A milestone was achieved in 2018 in the democratic journey of the country when it experienced the first successful and peaceful transition of power in Bishkek from one elected government to the next elected government. Its neighbour Tajikistan, soon after the independence, faced security challenges in the form of half a decade long civil war (1992-97). After that, the country initiated economic reforms. Uzbekistan focused on stability within the country and in the region. It faced the security challenges emanating from the neighbouring Afghanistan. Turkmenistan adopted the policy of 'permanent neutrality' and pursued natural resource exploitation for economic development.

In order to engage with the wider world, the Central Asian countries adopted 'multi-vector' foreign policy in pursuance of their national interests. In this framework, they cooperated with major powers of the world besides maintaining close relations with Russia. Following the 9/11 attacks in the US, Central Asian countries cooperated in the military operations led by the US against Afghanistan. Certain Central Asian republics even allowed military bases of various countries in their territories. However, now only two countries in the region have foreign military presence in the form of Russian forces. The Central Asian republics also endorse China's Belt and Road Initiative (BRI) and the region is considered an important component of the project. Countries of the region are also developing framework for cooperation with NATO's partnership initiatives. Though the republics in the region adopted different growth path suitable to their interest and requirements, India has successfully maintained good relations with all the five.

If we see the phases of development in Central Asia it becomes clear that in the initial phase or in the first decade the Republics focused on internal stability and development. During the next ten years starting with the new millennium, security consideration remained the driving factor for these republics, especially with regard to the situation in Afghanistan and three republics sharing boundary with that country. The third decade, which roughly began in early 2010, brought connectivity in greater attention to the republics. China launched the BRI, roads were built, railway lines were constructed, and pipelines were laid down. Russia along with Kazakhstan launched the Eurasian Economic Union (EEU). Now, the Central Asian republics have stabilized and connected internally and with the outside world. The regional cooperation mechanism is shaping up. Two rounds of consultative summits of Central Asian leaders have been held in Nursultan and Tashkent in 2018 and 2019 respectively. The Tashkent document says it is not aimed against interests of any third party but aspires to increase regional cooperation and coordination (MFA, 2019). They resorted to deepening their cooperation with regional and extra-regional powers, including through the Shanghai Cooperation Organisation (SCO).

India has been seen as a natural partner by the Central Asian countries in their process of development. The relationship at the bilateral levels and at the regional levels between India and the region of Central Asia is getting stronger and diverse. The region was considered as India's neighbourhood and keeping the new geography in mind, an extended neighbourhood. The relationship further evolved into partnership and three of the five republics are India's strategic partners.

Nonetheless, despite sharing good political relations between India and republics of Central Asia and existence of mutual cooperation potential, trade and economic relations have been below the desired level. It is considered that Central Asia being landlocked and the lack of direct land connectivity have been hampering trade ties with the region. The problem can be addressed only through multilateral level by engaging with other regional countries at various economic and connectivity initiatives aimed towards the region.

A major initiative to engage with the region at the regional and multilateral level came from India in the form of 'Connect India-Central Asia' Policy, 2012. On the occasion of two decades of engagement with Central Asia, the policy document was released. The 'Connect Central Asia' policy envisages to 'interact closely' with the region both at bilateral as well as multilateral levels. It was announced during the first track II India-Central Asia Dialogue held at Bishkek in 2012. The track II Dialogue has since evolved as an important engaging platform bringing academia, officials and business leaders from five republics and India together to discuss and strengthen mutual cooperation in various fields, including in security and culture.

India's multilateral approach in deepening ties with the region was also evident during the visit by Prime Minister Narendra Modi to Central Asia in July 2015. By visiting all the five republics in a single visit, Prime Minister Modi indicated that India is envisaging a pan-region engagement in the neighbourhood. The visit reinvigorated the ties with the Republics. During the visit, various documents consisting of cooperation in different areas were signed, including energy, defence and military, tourism, railways, science and technology, culture and sports (Zafar, 2016).

The recent years have seen much more progress at the multilateral level engagement between India and Central Asia at various fora. India is now a full member of the Shanghai Cooperation Organization (SCO). After joining the organization in 2017, for the first time, the country attended the Qingdao Summit in 2018. India had been an observer with the organization for a long time. SCO is an active organization and regular engagements are organized at various levels throughout the year. It can be said that both Russia and China have been successful in deepening cooperation with republics of the region through SCO platform. India's candidature for full membership was supported by all Central Asian countries that are members of the Organization. The republics consider India to be a positive contributor to SCO objectives and processes.

India's engagement with its neighbouring region of Central Asia has gathered some pace on the front of economic cooperation. The momentum has been provided by growing connectivity with and within the Eurasian region. Countries of the region, especially Uzbekistan have taken initiatives to increase connections with other neighbours and with Afghanistan. New Delhi has become a party to the inter-region Ashgabat Agreement, which provides for a connectivity corridor between Central Asia and West Asia, giving Central Asia an opening to the Indian Ocean and West Asia a corridor to Eurasian landmass. Further, India has also ratified the TIR convention in 2017, which allows easier movement of goods in sealed containers among the signatory countries.

Apart from policy measures and providing lead and political frameworks, New Delhi is also engaged in creating novel multilateral connectivity and energy infrastructure links between South Asia and Central Asia, and further to Eurasia. The International North- South Transport Corridor (INSTC) is making progress in its implementation. It is a shorter and more feasible route from India to connect with Central Asia and Eurasia. Running along the north-south axis, the multimodal transportation network links the Indian Ocean to Russia through Iran and Europe.

In order to complete the connectivity network and making

them more feasible, India is making substantial investments in the Iranian port of Chabahar. This port could be the shortest distance route from Central Asia to the open seas. India is also engaged in the construction of a rail line from Chabahar port to link it to the Iranian railway network at Zahedan, which will greatly ease movement of cargo. India is playing an important role in developing infrastructure in Afghanistan and has already constructed 218 km. long Zeranj-Delaram road in the country, which links it to neighbouring Iranian road network.

India is a fast growing economy and it needs uninterrupted supply of affordable energy resources. Turkmenistan and other republics of the region have abundant gas and other sources of energy, include uranium and hydropower.

The Turkmenistan-Afghanistan-Pakistan-India (TAPI) natural gas pipeline is a multilateral cooperation initiative aimed at energy resources utilization. It can be a good example of reciprocity where the supplier gets market for long-term supply and the purchaser secures supply from new areas. In recent months, the pipeline has made some significant progress, including commencement of construction activities in Turkmenistan and works in Afghanistan. Reportedly, security of the pipeline for the section passing from Afghanistan has been assured by Taliban (Ghubar, 2018). TAPI, however, still has to be seen operational on the ground.

Recent Developments

After about three decades of engagement with Central Asia, India launched another initiative aimed at growing multilateral cooperation with the region. The most recent initiative by New Delhi to increase political and other interactions has been the first ministerial level India-Central Asia Dialogue held in January 2019. The Foreign Ministers' dialogue was held in the ancient Silk Route city of Samarqand in Uzbekistan. India's External Affairs Minister Ms. Sushma Swaraj and Mr. Abdulaziz Kamilov, Foreign Minister of Uzbekistan, were the co-chairs of the two-day Dialogue. Foreign Ministers Mr. Sirojiddin

Muhriddin from Tajikistan, Mr. Chingiz Aidarbekov from Kyrgyz Republic and Mr. Rashid Meredov from Turkmenistan attended the programme. Kazakhstan was represented by First Deputy Minister of Foreign Affairs Mr. Mukhtar Tileuberdi. Besides, Foreign Minister of Afghanistan Mr. Salahuddin Rabbani was also present as a special invitee in the Session on connectivity issues in the region.

The First India-Central Asia Dialogue at the Foreign Ministers' level can be considered a historic development in inter-region relations. India announced a number of measures aimed at improving business and commerce relations with the neighbourhood region. At the governmental level from the two sides, an 'India-Central Asia Development Group' has been proposed in order to explore development partnership between India and the region. To improve connectivity at the business level, an 'India-Central Asia Business Council' has also been established. The Council aims to promote business as well as to study the viability of creating air corridors between India and the region for trade in agricultural produce, food items and perishable products (FICCI, 2020). The initiatives seem timely as the connectivity through various land routes are becoming operational and it is time that business community from two sides increase their interactions and explore possible areas of cooperation.

The Dialogue also focused on cultural exchanges between the two sides. To improve cultural connectivity, it was mentioned that Indian Council for Cultural Relations (ICCR) would organize an international conference in India on cultural connections with the region. The Central Asian Republics need assistance in capacity building. In this area, India offered special training courses for persons from the region in prevention of drug smuggling, remote sensing, IT, film, and oil and gas sector. India proposed to send 10 English teachers to Five Republics. Besides, two-week training for eight diplomats from every Central Asian country has been offered at the Foreign Service Institute in New Delhi. India proposed an annual hosting of a media delegation of five each from Central Asian countries. It will help in increasing awareness about each other among the common people.

The inclusion of Afghanistan in Dialogue was perhaps aimed to restore the country as a link between the two regions of Central Asia and South Asia. It is expected that economic integration of Afghanistan with the economies of South Asia and Central Asia would contribute to bringing peace and stability in the country. Afghanistan provides crucial land link between the Indian subcontinent and Central Asia-Eurasia. The country is also a member of South Asian Association for Regional Cooperation (SAARC).

The country has the potential to once again play its historical role of an enabler in inter-region trade and economic relations. Logically, Afghanistan finds a place in larger policy framework of India's engagement with Central Asia and Eurasia. India's engagement with the region is all set to increase substantially. Similarly, the situation in Afghanistan seems on the cusp of transformation.

India-Central Asia People-to-People Connections

As stated above, there is diversified and long running cultural affinity between the people of India and Central Asia. Many students from India go to Central Asian republics to pursue their education in medical and other courses and students from the region come to study in Indian institutions. Indian visual arts, including cinema and television serials are quite popular across the region. Yoga is becoming quite popular among various sections of the society in all republics.

Tourism and medical tourism has great potential for India and Central Asian countries. The recent initiative of Uzbekistan and Kazakhstan to create a common visa for the region can prove to be a landmark in regional cooperation if other republics also become party to it. A common visa for the entire region would give a much-needed fillip to tourism and investment in the region, including from India.

Similarly, there should be greater exchange of scholars,

students, professionals and ideas between the two regions. Literary masterpiece *Tuzuk-e Babari* is completing 500 years, which in a way has been associated with Kyrgyz people as well. Scholars from the region and India can explore studying the societies in the present context and compare it with the situation mentioned in the book by Babar.

Conclusion

India and the five Central Asian countries are potential natural partners in the region destined to come closer and increase their cooperation for the benefit of the people in South Asia and Central Asia. After the initial difficulties, India is now willing to develop closer relations in all areas, including political, economic, cultural and technology fields. If cultural, linguistic and historical connections bound the two sides in the past; in the contemporary times, economy, energy security and connectivity for commerce are the prime vectors bringing them to embrace each other.

Central Asia consists of vast territory but relatively small population. The potential of this region will be utilized more appropriately only when the states are politically and economically engaged not only at the bilateral levels but also at the multilateral fora. The landlocked status of Central Asia makes it imperative to develop relations with all serious stakeholders in the region, including India. India also showed its intent to further deepen engagement by holding the first India-Central Asia Dialogue at the Foreign Ministers' level in Uzbekistan in January 2019. Seemingly, a new chapter is about to begin in the India-Central Asia relations which will be significantly facilitated and contributed by the multilateral engagement.

References

Arun, S. (2017), "Russia: A Forgotten Trade Partner?", *The Hindu,* available at:
https://www.thehindu.com/business/Economy/russia-a-forgotten-trade-partner/article17898013.ece.

BBC (2017), "Kyrgyzstan Election: Sooronbay Jeenbekov Wins Historic Election", *BBC News,* available at:

https://www.bbc.com/news/world-asia-41625540.

FICCI (2020), "India-Central Asia Business Council was Launched", *The Federation of Indian Chambers of Commerce and Industry*, available at:
http://ficci.in/ficci-in-news-page.asp?nid=20394.

Ghubar, G. (2018), "Enhanced Security Measures in Effect for TAPI Pipeline", *Tolo News,* available at:
https://www.tolonews.com/afghanistan/enhanced-security-measures-effect-tapi-pipeline.

Ministry of External Affairs, Government of India, "Address by Prime Minister at Nazarbayev University, Astana, Kazakhstan", July 7, 2015, available at:
https://www.mea.gov.in/SpeechesStatements.htm?dtl/25436/Address_by_Prime_Minister_at_Nazarbayev_University_Astana_Kazakhstan.

Ministry of Foreign Affairs of Uzbekistan, "Joint Statement of the Consultative Meeting of the Heads of States of Central Asia", November 30, 2019, available at:
http://www.uzbekembassy.in/joint-statement-of-the-consultative-meeting-of-the-heads-of-states-of-central-asia

Moon, V. and Narake, H. (eds.) (2014), "Dr. Babasaheb Ambedkar Writings and Speeches", Vol. 3, Dr. Ambedkar Foundation, Ministry of Social Justice and Empowerment, Government of India, available at:
https://www.mea.gov.in/Images/attach/amb/Volume_03.pdf.

Mukherjee, B. (2014), "International Recognition of India's World Heritage: New, Exciting Projects on Anvil", Ministry of External Affairs, Government of India, available at:
https://www.mea.gov.in/in-focus
article.htm?23601/International+recognition+of+Indias+world+heritage++New+exciting+projects+n+anvil.

Thakur, J. (2015), "India Aims to Revive 'Cotton Route' to Counter Chinese Silk Route", *Hindustan Times*, Kolkata, available at:
http://iora.ris.org.in/sites/default/files/Hindustan_Times_Kolkata2015-03-26_page4.pdf.

Thapar, Romila (2000), "A History of India", Vol. 1, (12th ed.), New Delhi: Penguin Books.

Zafar, A. (2016), "PM Modi's Visit Reinvigorates Ties with Central Asia", Sapru House Paper, available at:
https://icwa.in/pdfs/shp/2014/sph2016.pdf.

2

India-Tajikistan Relations: Vistas for Increasing Engagement

Anirban Chatterjee

Introduction

India and Tajikistan relations are age old and time tested. The relationship can be traced back to the days of Kushana and Persian empires when Tajikistan was closely linked to Indian subcontinent (Gupta, 2019: 4). The historical contact between the two countries goes back to the ancient times. Zoroastrianism, Buddhism, Islam and Sufism played an important role in religio-cultural exchange between the two countries. In the medieval period, the relationship got further cemented through close cultural and linguistic interactions which continue even to this day.

Scholars, literati, spiritualists, traders, craftsmen and artists between the two countries always kept the door of interaction open. This enabled exchange of ideas, movement of goods, cultural interaction which in turned helped in emboldening people to people connect (Warikoo, 2016). Indian poets like Amir Khusrao, Ghani Kashmiri and Saadi of Iran have exerted great influence in so far as Tajik literature and culture are concerned. The Pamiri language has close resemblance to that of classical Sanskrit language, and the Indo-Aryan group of language has close affinity with the Tajik language (Warikoo, 2016).

During the Soviet times, India's relations with Tajikistan were routed through Moscow. Tajikistan emerged as a sovereign independent nation after the dissolution of USSR. Tajikistan is a landlocked small country situated in the Central Asian region. On the south, Tajikistan is bordered by

Afghanistan, Kyrgyzstan to the North, China to the east and Uzbekistan to the west. Tajikistan's close proximity to Pakistan Occupied Kashmir (PoK) is important from India's perspective. India was one among the first countries to have recognized Tajikistan's independence after the demise of USSR in 1991. Immediately after its independence, Tajikistan plunged into a civil war which lasted for five years. As a result, Tajikistan's economy and social conditions got aggravated. The bilateral relationship did not take off well in the critical years of Civil War. However, in the last few years, the relationship has been strengthened and the two countries are exploring newer areas to expand their engagement.

Political and Diplomatic Relations

The two countries established their diplomatic relations in August 1992 (Bakshi, 2013). The bilateral relationship between the two countries has been marked by frequent high-level visits and regular diplomatic exchanges. Although, successive Indian governments highlighted the importance of the region, but India's presence in the region was below expectations. The region got a major fillip from the Indian side when PM Modi toured the five Central Asian countries in 2015. This was unprecedented in the sense that never did an Indian PM visit all the Central Asian states ever at one stroke. It underlines the importance of the region in India's foreign policy endeavour under the Modi government.

It also marks a major breakthrough in terms of re-orienting India's foreign policy towards Eurasia in general and Central Asia in particular. During his visit to Tajikistan, PM Modi discussed with the Tajik side, ways to increase engagement between the two countries. It was decided that both countries will expand cooperation in defence, connectivity and fighting terrorism. At the summit meeting of Shanghai Cooperation Organisation (SCO) held in 2016, Indian PM met with Tajik President Emomali Rahmon. On the invitation of PM Modi, the Tajik president subsequently visited India and the bilateral relations were thoroughly reviewed. During the 18th SCO summit meeting held in Chinese city of Qingdao in 2018, both the leaders took stock of the two countries' relationship, especially the political and security aspects (Gupta, 2019: 5).

From the Tajik side, the incumbent president Rahmon visited India six times: 1995, 1999, 2001, 2006, 2012, and 2016. The Foreign Minister and the Defence Minister of Tajikistan visited India in May 2015 and January 2018 respectively.

From the Indian side, former PM Atal Bihari Vajpayee paid a visit to Tajikistan in 2003, President Ms. Pratibha Devisingh Patil visited in 2009, Vice President Shri Hamid Ansari visited in 2013, Foreign Minister Smt. Sushma Swaraj visited in September 2014, Prime Minister Modi visited Tajikistan in 2015, and President Ram Nath Kovind visited in 2018 (MEA, 2018: 1-2).

The increasing cooperation between the two countries is due to the convergence of economic, security and cultural interests. Frequent high level visits have augmented political and diplomatic relations. The two countries' bilateral relationship is being etched out by four important consultative mechanisms through which the bilateral relationship is deliberated upon (MEA, 2018: 2):

Foreign Office Consultations (FOC): Held four rounds of talk and the last one was held in New Delhi in 2018.

Joint Working Group on Counter-terrorism: Held three rounds of talk and the last round was held in the Tajik capital, Dushanbe in 2017.

Joint Commission on Trade, Economic, Scientific and Technical Cooperation: Tenth session of deliberation happened in January 2019 in Dushanbe.

Joint Working Group on Defence Cooperation: Held its seventh meeting in Dushanbe on July 26-27, 2018.

In each of these meetings, the whole gamut of the two countries' relationship was reviewed and deliberated upon. Both agreed to enhance cooperation in all of these areas in order to take the relationship one step further. Tajikistan supported India's full membership in SCO, and it has also been an advocate of India's permanent membership in the United Nations Security Council (UNSC). On the other hand, India supported Tajikistan's accession to World Trade Organization (WTO) in 2013, and also supported the candidature of Tajikistan in The Economic and Social Council (ECOSOC) (MEA, 2018: 6). The visit by Indian Prime Minister Shri Narendra Modi to Tajikistan in 2015 laid emphasis to re-kindle the old civilizational and cultural connection with the region. During the visit of PM Modi, the two countries inked a host of agreements to augment ties in the fields of education and culture.

The two countries inked three important agreements during Tajik president's visit to India in 2016: to cooperate in combating terrorism and extremism, to exchange financial intelligence regarding money laundering and financing of terror, and the last one pertaining to avoidance of double taxation agreement to ease business between the two countries. To smoothen economic partnership between the two countries, the possibility of signing a Bilateral Investment Treaty was also discussed in the meeting. The bilateral relations were taken further during the visit of Indian President Ram Nath Kovind to Tajikistan in 2018 in which MoU and agreements on fields such as space technology, renewable energy, disaster management, youth affairs, agricultural research and education and research on traditional medicine were inked (MEA, 2018: 2).

Trade and Economic Relations

In case of bilateral trade, Indian exports to Tajikistan consists of pharmaceuticals, clothing and apparel, accessories, machinery, handicraft, meat and meat products. Tajikistan's exports to India comprises of different kinds of slag, ores and ash, organic chemicals, aluminium, cotton, herbal oil and dry fruits. Bilateral trade between the two countries is still below the potential. The absence of direct land connectivity between

India and Tajikistan is said to be one of the stumbling blocks for cementing strong trade ties between the two countries. The presence of Pakistan in between India and Tajikistan further complicates the trade ties as Pakistan does not allow the movement of goods and cargoes from India through its territory. As a result of this, the trade takes place through sea route which is tortuous. The trade takes place from India to Bandar Abbas port in Iran via sea and from Bandar Abbas via Turkmenistan and Uzbekistan through land and then to Tajikistan for the transportation of goods. Trade between the two countries is in favour of India (Sajjanhar, 2016).

The trade statistics of last seven years between the two countries would better explicate the overall trade scenario (Tables 2.1 and 2.2).

Table 2.1: Indian Exports to Tajikistan

(Value in US$ Million)

2011-12	2012-13	2013-14	2014-15	2015-16	2016-17	2017-18
21.28	35.16	54.27	53.71	22.26	20.44	23.94

Source: Department of Commerce, Government of India.

Table 2.2: Indian Imports from Tajikistan

(Value in US$ Million)

2011-12	2012-13	2013-14	2014-15	2015-16	2016-17	2017-18
8.86	12.86	0.86	4.39	9.98	21.82	50.29

Source: Department of Commerce, Government of India.

As per Tajik data, Tajikistan's total export in 2017 was US$ 1.12 billion. As per Tajik data, Tajikistan's total import in 2017 was US$ 2.78 billion.

Strategic and Security Relations

As already mentioned, Tajikistan's geo-strategic location is of considerable importance for India. The adoption of 'Connect Central Asia' policy by India in 2012 is a recognition of the fact that India's strategic interests are growing in the region. In addition to sharing border with Uzbekistan, China and Kyrgyzstan, Tajikistan shares 1,400 km. long porous border with Afghanistan. It is situated in the propinquity of PoK. It assumes a significant place in India's foreign and security policy matrix, especially in the case of Pakistan and Afghanistan (Roy, 2012). The long presence of Taliban in the region since 1990s, and the continued support to it by Pakistan's Inter Service Intelligence (ISI) are of significant security concerns for India in forging closer ties with Tajikistan. The confluence of two countries' interests can be seen in the 1990s when both India and Tajikistan extended their support to the *Northern Alliance* in fighting Taliban (Gupta, 2019: 8).

Both the countries acknowledge the threats posed by radical and extremist forces in the region in disrupting the social fabric. The calculations of the security implications by both the countries bring them closer to each other in jointly collaborating to fight the menace of terrorism and extremism. The fall of Afghanistan into the hands of extremist forces will have grave security consequences for Tajikistan as it shares border with Afghanistan. It will subsequently have spill over impact in the entire Central Asian region. Likewise, it can have strategic fall out for India's interests in Afghanistan. It may threaten to disrupt India's developmental activities where India has huge investments. The penetration of radical elements in Tajikistan may have grave consequences for India in so far as security is concerned because of its propinquity to PoK and its probable impact on an already precarious security scenario in the Indian state of Jammu and Kashmir (Roy, 2012).

During the visit of Tajik president to India in 2012, the bilateral relations between the two countries were elevated to the level of 'strategic partnership' keeping in mind the increasing engagement between the two countries. In the Joint Statement issued by both the governments, it was highlighted that the two countries have "decided to elevate their bilateral relations to the level of a long-term strategic partnership". The strategic partnership will be multifarious in nature encompassing cooperation in the realms of political, economic, human development, defence, counter terrorism, science and technology, tourism and culture. The visit of Tajikistan's president was analysed in India's defence and security circles as an important one in the wake of the two countries' existing relationship and the positive outcome of the relationship emerging out of the strategic partnership signed by them. The visit was also seen by some strategic analysts as an attempt by India to give prominence to Tajikistan in so far as its foreign policy towards Central Asia is concerned (Roy, 2012).

Pakistan has long been accused of harbouring and sheltering radical outfits in both within its territory and beyond in attaining its twin objectives of gaining strategic depth in Afghanistan and destabilizing the state of Jammu and Kashmir. The re-surfacing of Taliban and its possible impact on Afghan peace process, US pulling out its forces from Afghanistan have significant security consequences for both Tajikistan and India. Against this backdrop, both the countries realize the exigency of mutual collaboration in dealing with the prevailing security challenges in the region (Gupta, 2019: 8). They have sought to collaborate in fighting the menace of terrorism and extremism by exchanging data, information finances and networks of terror outfits. Both the countries' security agencies aim to buttress their efforts through frequent dialogue and deliberation. The two countries' Foreign Offices are being briefed about such dialogues involving crucial security aspects. The Joint Working Groups on Defence Cooperation and Counter Terrorism provide rational framework to augment cooperation in this regard.

India helped Tajikistan by spending US$ 70 million in the up-gradation of Ayni air base located near the capital. It is now operational. The Chinese and Pakistani media have tried to portray this attempt of India to get 'strategic foothold' in the region through its military presence. The Russian government also came out criticizing this move of India (Putz, 2015).

However, the Tajik government made it quite clear that India will not use the airport for military purpose. Besides the Ayni airbase, India has also refurbished the Farkhor airbase. The refurbishment of these two airbases is symptomatic of India's growing security engagement with Tajikistan. Having two airbases in Tajikistan is also a testimony of Tajikistan's strategic significance from Indian perspective (Mullen and Prasad, 2014).

The state of the art airport with advanced technology and upgraded facilities at Ayni is approximately 3,200 meters and is equipped for the landing of all kinds of aircraft. During his visit to Tajikistan in 2018, President Ram Nath Kovind went to Ayni airbase which is indicative of India's growing presence in the base. The president met with the Indian Air Force contingent posted at the airbase. This airbase holds strategic importance for India in the backdrop of its inclusion in the SCO and the ongoing efforts to stabilize Afghanistan by working together with Central Asian states and Russia within the framework of joint counter terrorism collaboration (Gupta, 2019: 9).

The defence cooperation between the two countries constitutes an important component of their bilateral relationship. A large number of Tajik military officers and cadets are being trained by India. National Defence College and Indian Military Academy provide the required military training. The India-Tajikistan Friendship hospital was set up by India near Qurganteppe. Medical staff and doctors from India are there to provide necessary medical care to armed and civilian patients. The contribution and support of India in the capacity building and infrastructural development of Tajikistan's defence and military sector is well appreciated by Tajikistan's president Rahmon.

Both the countries pay due attention to the disruption of regional peace and security caused by forces of religious fundamentalism, terrorism and radicalism. Taking stock of the situation, President of India during his visit to Tajikistan in

2018 accorded highest priority to increasing cooperation in order to exterminate terrorism in all its forms and expression. The Tajik President and Indian President condemned the sponsoring, financing and providing shelter to terrorists and extremist forces. In order to concretize their joint fight against terrorism, both the countries decided to adopt the United Nation General Assembly (UNGA) approved '*Comprehensive Convention on International Terrorism*' by laying stress on the commitment to fight the three evil forces of extremism, terrorism and radicalism. In order to materialize this, stress was given to augment cooperation between the two countries' security councils and agencies.

The sustained cooperation in the defence sector lays bare the commitment of the two countries in ensuring regional peace and security. The meeting of Joint Working Group on Defence Cooperation which took place on July 26, 2018 in Dushanbe is a pointer to that direction.

The convergence of their interests can also be seen in the context of Afghanistan reconstruction process which complements their bilateral relations. Both the countries are in favour of Afghanistan initiated, Afghan led, Afghan managed peace process which is representative of all sections of Afghan society. Given the precarious situation in Afghanistan, and the fragile peace and security scenario, both the countries give stress to the fact of increasing bilateral engagement and multilateral collaboration in stabilizing the situation in Afghanistan. The kind of developmental and humanitarian works that India has undertaken in Afghanistan from capacity building to developing economic and social infrastructure, building of parliamentary institution and human development has been praised by the Tajik president (Gupta, 2019: 11).

The presence of extremist forces in Pakistan and Afghanistan and their possible spill over in Central Asia via Tajikistan has always been a point of concern for both India and Tajikistan since the heydays of Taliban. The withdrawal of US led NATO forces in 2014 has created a security vacuum in the region. The re-emergence of Taliban with the backing of Pakistan army and ISI has complicated the scenario which has brought importance to the notion of collective security in the deliberations of India and Tajikistan. It can aggravate further with Pakistan continuing to support militants who have cross border linkages with Hizb-ut-Tahrir (HT) and Islamic Movement of Uzbekistan (IMU) in Central Asia.

This makes Tajikistan more susceptible as it shares border with Afghanistan and its close proximity to Pakistan (Warikoo, 2015). The threat of ISIS has also been taken into account. The presence and expansion of Al-Qaeda from Afghanistan to Pakistan and finally to Central Asia is a point to reckon with. It is widely known that all these terror groups are intertwined with each other. Al-Qaeda claims to be present in the Indian subcontinent which is a serious security challenge for India. In wake of this, it is imperative for both the countries to take stock of the impending security challenge and to act in a coordinated manner to thwart terrorism and extremism.

The defence mechanism of Tajikistan is not well equipped to tackle a challenge of this magnitude which defines why both the countries should closely cooperate with each other. Although, Russian forces are present on the Tajik-Afghan border through an agreement between Russian Federation and Tajikistan to protect the latter's border in order to keep its territory safe from these extremist forces, however, the deeper security engagement between India and Tajikistan will have more meaningful outcome in combating terrorism and the threats emanating from it.

Although, Tajikistan is not endowed with oil and natural gas, as other Central Asian countries like Uzbekistan and Kazakhstan are, however, Tajikistan is enriched with water resources. Sixty percent of water supply in Central Asia is channelled through Tajikistan's water reservoirs (Sajjanhar, 2016). Tajikistan's strategic significance gets multiplied because of it being a major hydroelectric power supplier in the region. Among the Commonwealth of Independent States

(CIS), Tajikistan is the second largest producer of hydroelectricity after Russia. Tajikistan also accounts for four percent of total water supply in the world. Many analysts have highlighted Tajikistan's hydroelectric potential which is estimated to be around 40,000 MW.

The Varzob-1 hydropower station has been renovated with India's assistance. Tajikistan's richness in hydropower resources prompted both the countries to increase cooperation in this lucrative sector. During the visit of India's Water Resource Minister Nitin Gadkari to Tajikistan in 2018, both sides agreed to strengthen their relationship in the economic sector with particular focus on cooperating in sustainable water development (Ministry of Water Resources, 2018). Besides, being a hydroelectric power, Tajikistan is also endowed with gold, stone and silver in addition to sizeable deposits of zinc, mercury and brown coal. The presence of these resources enhances Tajikistan's strategic importance for India to forge closer ties (Roy, 2012).

Connect Central Asia Policy for Stronger Ties

The 'Connect Central Asia' policy of India mooted by Minister of State for External Affairs E. Ahmad in 2012 as part of Track Two Initiative was meant to augment India's relations with the region by collaborating in number of areas: from setting up information technology centres, universities, hospitals, an e-network for telemedicine, undertaking joint economic initiatives, strengthening trade and commerce, ameliorating air connectivity, bolstering tourism, augmenting strategic partnership in security and defence sectors and joint scientific research (Roy, 2012).

The importance of 'connectivity' in an era of economic interdependence has never been felt as acutely as in recent times. It is even more pertinent for one of the fastest growing but energy deficient economies like India to tap the potential of connectivity to meet its domestic requirements. As a result, the country is increasing engagement with the neighbouring regions, particularly Central Asia. The importance of national energy security is manifest in the fact that India has surpassed Japan to become world's third largest consumer of oil (The Hindu, 2016).

In order to expedite its market diversification strategy to encourage exporters to reduce their dependence on traditional markets in the West, where there is not much demand at present, India has pitched for fast tracking the operationalization of INSTC to significantly reduce the cost and travel time, and also to gain access to the markets of Central Asian countries and reach even beyond. In the wake of this, the accession of India in Ashgabat Agreement is seen to be promoting and facilitating connectivity between India and Central Asian countries including Tajikistan (Sajjanhar, 2016). India's growing bilateral relations with the countries in the region is a pointer in that direction.

In the wake of Prime Minister Modi's visit to five Central Asian countries in 2015, it became apparent that the importance India gives to the region can't be understated. Modi's statement at the Ufa Summit in 2015 is a testimony of India's growing interest and desire to become a player in the region, which can be illustrated in his speech, "As we look forward, we would lend our support to improving transportation and communication networks in the region. We can create a vast network of physical and digital connectivity that extends from Eurasia's northern corner to Asia's southern shores. The International North-South Transportation Corridor is a step in that direction" (Roy, 2015).

Culture and Tourism

The image of India in Tajikistan is positive. The Tajik public opinion is in favour of India. It is due to seamless people to people contact since ancient times which the successive Indian and Tajikistan governments have laid stress on. India wields considerable influence in Tajikistan due to its soft power capacity. Indian films and TV serials are frequently dubbed in Tajik language which is appreciated by the people of Tajikistan. The dubbing is possible because in most of the Tajik universities, Hindi and Urdu departments are present, which is indicative of the popularity of India among young scholars in Tajikistan to learn Indian culture and history through Indian languages (Mullen and Prasad, 2014). The Embassy of India has inaugurated couple of Study Corners on India in prominent Tajik institutions and universities which will further spurt the cultural relations between the two countries.

The cultural relations between the two countries are product of shared historical legacy. The famous Tajik poet Mirzo Tursunzade wrote a volley of poems on India during his visit to the country in 1947. It was the year in which India liberated itself from the clutches of British colonialism as a result of which his poem encouraged Tajik students to study about India. Similarly, the influence of Indian writers and poets has had a considerable influence among Tajik people. The translations of the works of Rabindranath Tagore, Munshi Prem Chand and others had an impact on Tajik society. After his visit to the then Soviet Union and his translated works in Tajik language, Tagore became a popular household name in USSR including Tajikistan (Mullen and Prasad, 2014).

The Indian Embassy in Tajikistan routinely organises various cultural programs to commemorate important events and festivals. Swami Vivekananda Cultural Centre was recently inaugurated by the Water Resources Minister Shri Nitin Gadkari. In the cultural centre, tabla, kathak, yoga and Sanskrit teachers appointed by ICCR alongside local teachers organise and perform cultural activities. ICCR funded cultural events take place not only in the Tajik capital but also in other cities as well. In 2017 and 2018, an art and cultural band of twenty people came to India in order to take part in the Surajkund Mela (MEA, 2018: 5).

The cooperation between the two countries can also be noticed in the tourism sector. A direct weekly flight from Dushanbe to Delhi is operational which was restarted by the

Tajik Air in May 2013. The resumption of direct flight connectivity will bolster business prospects. It is also reported that medical tourism is on the rise. The visa regimes between the two countries are liberal. In a day or two visas are issued to the nationals. From Tajikistan, the bulk of the people travel to India on e-visa for the purpose of medical treatment or tourism. Until recently, Tajikistan has opened the facility of online visa regime for people of India. This will encourage travellers from India to travel to Tajikistan.

Concluding Observations

India-Tajikistan relations are multi-pronged and multidimensional. It is an outcome of close historical interaction, cultural connection and mutual trust. The geo-strategic location of Tajikistan holds key for India to increase its presence in the region. Even though India's presence can be seen in the region, but it needs to adopt a more pro-active role in terms of engaging with the region in a more sustained, strategic and economic terms. In 2017, both sides commemorated the 25th anniversary of their diplomatic relations and pledged to carry forward their engagements in a more robust way. At the bilateral level, frequent high level visits have laid the ground for deeper cooperation.

The bilateral trade between the two countries is below expectations due to the absence of direct surface connectivity which needs a booster. The Central Asian region is a landlocked region—the initiation of connectivity projects has the potential to transform the region into a major economic hub in the world as Central Asia is endowed with natural and energy resources and is located at a critical geo-political hotspot in the world. India's effort in building the Chabahar Port as part of the INSTC, and many upcoming projects will enhance the strategic importance of the region and will open great opportunity for India. India's membership of the SCO, and its amicable bilateral relations with every Central Asian country including Tajikistan are a testimony of the fact that

India will be benefited from the efforts undertaken.

The critical geo-strategic location of Tajikistan and the precarious security scenario in the region demand closer cooperation between the two countries. Drug trafficking, extremism, cross-border terror networks and money laundering are some of the issues plaguing the region. The fragile political situation in Afghanistan and the impending peace process with a resurgent Taliban backed by Pakistan, complicate the security scenario further. The outcome of the Afghan peace process will be felt by both India and Tajikistan. The proximity of Tajikistan to PoK is a point of concern for India which requires sustained dialogue and deliberation between the two countries at all levels. The region throws great opportunities for India as well as some challenges. Handling the challenges requires broader engagements with all the Central Asian countries including Tajikistan which share more or less the same concerns.

References

Bilateral Brief on "India-Tajikistan Bilateral Relations", Ministry of External Affairs, Government of India, December 31, 2018, available at: https://mea.gov.in/Portal/ForeignRelation/Bilateral_Brief_India_Tajik_dec_2018.pdf.

Press Information Bureau, Ministry of Water Resources, Government of India, June 21, 2018, available at: http://pib.gov.in/newsite/PrintRelease.aspx?relid=180091.

"India Becomes Third Largest Oil Consumer", *The Hindu,* June 8, 2016, available at: https://www.thehindu.com/business/Industry/India-becomes-third-largest-oil-consumer/article14391860.ece.

Bakshi, J. (2013), "India and Tajikistan: Common Concerns and Shared Interests in Evolving Regional Geopolitics", in Jyotsna Bakhshi (ed.), 'Geo-political Dynamics in India-Tajikistan Relations', Pentagon Press.

Gupta, Pravesh Kumar (2019), "India-Tajikistan Relations: The Security Factor", VIF Brief, March 2019, Vivekananda International Foundation.

Mullen AND Prasad (2014), "India-Tajikistan Brief", Centre for Policy Research, available at: https://www.cprindia.org/sites/default/files/policy-briefs/India-Tajikistan%20Brief%20Final.pdf.

Putz, Catherine (2015), "Will There Be An Indian Air Base in Tajikistan?", *The Diplomat*, available at: https://thediplomat.com/2015/07/will-there-be-an-indian-air-base-in-tajikistan.

Roy, Meena Singh (2012), "India and Tajikistan: Building a Long-term Strategic Partnership", Institute for Defence Studies and Analyses, available at: https://idsa.in/idsacomments/IndiaandTajikistanBuildingalongtermStrategicPartnership_MeenaSRoy_180912.

Sajjanhar, A. (2016), "Tajikistan President Visits India; Gives Big Impetus to Bilateral Ties", Observer Research Foundation, available at: https://www.orfonline.org/expert-speak/tajikistan-president-visits-india-impetus-bilateral-ties.

Warikoo, K. (2015), "Afghanistan Factor in Tajikistan Crisis, 1991-1997", in K. Warikoo and Kh. Umarov (eds.), "Tajikistan in the 21st Century: Society, Politics and Economy", Pentagon Press.

Warikoo, K. (2016), "Revitalizing India-Tajikistan Relations", *Himalayan and Central Asian Studies*, 20(2-3).

3

Humanitarian Co-operation of India in Central Asia in the Context of Soft Power

Edilbekuulu Syimyk

Introduction

With increasing globalization, many obsolete means of conducting foreign policy have faded into the background. In the 21st century, soft power has started to acquire greater significance and in almost every case, proving its effectiveness. In this regard, the foreign policy of India, an aspiring great power, is very relevant. Modern India is a state with an exceptionally solid arsenal of cultural weapons. This factor certainly allows India to widely and actively use soft power to increase its prosperity. These circumstances determine the relevance of the study. The term soft power was first introduced into scientific use by an American analyst, Joseph Nay in 1990 in a published book entitled "A Call to Leadership: The Changing Nature of American Power", in which he viewed soft power as a means of achieving specific goals through voluntary participation, attractiveness and sympathy (Nye, J., 1991, 2004). If supporters of hard power as a tool, rely on military power and economic conditions, then the means of soft power are the culture, political values and realized foreign policy of a given state (Minasyan, N., 2017).

India's Soft Power Approach

India as an independent country was founded in 1947 with liberation from British colonialism. Since then, Indian leadership has repeatedly revised its foreign policy. It is noteworthy that soft power was used immediately after the proclamation of India as a sovereign state, and that the ideology of Indian style soft power, developed during the second half of the 20th century. Jacques Hymans argues that one can imagine colonial India by comparing it to the British Empire within the framework of three dichotomies that reveal the cultural code of the nation: male and female, adult and child; man and the beast. The British Empire was seen as a state with pronounced signs of masculinity and strength, maturity and civilization, while India seemed to be the antithesis of civilized society (Jacques, E.C., 2009).

Indian soft power has gone through three stages of development. The first, which began in 1947 and ended with the death of the first Prime Minister of India, Jawaharlal Nehru in 1964, was characterized by a clear commitment to employing soft power in their foreign policy. During the second period, which lasted from 1964 to 1998, India almost entirely relied on hard power. Finally, the third period in the history of modern India (from 1998 to the present) is conditionally characterized by the purposeful efforts of the Indian leadership to incorporate a smart power strategy into its foreign policy.

The main slogan of soft power in India's foreign policy is the statement "the strength of the argument against the argument of force", which clearly shows the principle of Indian pragmatic philosophy of ahimsa (non-violence). After its wars with Pakistan and China, India openly tried to advocate non-violence to the world. However, Indian non-violence did not work with China. Post-war, India first developed a nuclear deterrent. India then started employing soft power to position itself as a peaceful power, which has developed consistently, following the path of Mahatma Gandhi. The legacy of Buddha, non-violence, traditional Indian philosophy, yoga, medicine, health practices and nutrition, and much more—all of these elements are sources of Indian soft power; there is growth potential in every one of these. Provided they have a focused strategy and adapt to modern realities, they can become powerful instruments of influence, since they are also elements of the world cultural heritage.

India is doing a lot to make its cultural values proliferate. One significant Indian cultural achievement has been the establishment of World Yoga Day. Prime Minister Narendra Modi often speaks about yoga—increasingly popularizing this cultural factor; in addition, he actively shares it on social network platforms such as Twitter and Facebook also. In the context of soft power, India, and the PRC belong to the countries of the "second wave" applying new humanitarian technologies. Therefore, they often face various problems associated with persistent stereotypes (non-observance of human rights, corruption, poor controllability, etc.), which often predominate negative information and form an aggressive image of a country that prefers rigid methods of influence and pressure on the world community.

India has certain advantages associated with various aspects of civilizational development, among which we can separately highlight the following:

1. Features of the eastern-intuitive style of thinking (image-sensual perception and an artistic vision of the world, special emotionality and integrity, originally inherent in the East), which helps Indian experts to effectively select and broadcast the appropriate images and meanings.
2. The scale of its cultural and historical heritage: this factor comes to the fore in modern soft power technologies, providing a serious competitive advantage.
3. The absence of a serious identity crisis, which makes it possible to most seriously focus on external communications.

India today has gone beyond leadership in South Asia. At the same time, in the world perception, India remains in the shadow of its more powerful neighbour China. This may be positive for New Delhi. For example, both countries possess nuclear weapons regardless of the NPT. However, the media often focuses on China's nuclear threat, while India's nuclear potential is less actively discussed, despite the fact that New Delhi, like Beijing, consistently criticizes the treaty, seeking recognition of its nuclear status.

Currently, India is actively promoting its national interests abroad by actively taking part in developing its infrastructure development portfolio. Wade Shepard notes that India has its own transcontinental strategy called the North-South Transport Corridor, which is a multimodal corridor of India with a total length of 7,200 kilometres (Shepard, W., 2017). This trade route from India to the Russian Federation connects the Indian Ocean, the Caspian Sea and the Persian Gulf. On these routes, goods will be delivered from the port of Jawaharlal Nehru and the port of Kandla in western India to the port of Bandar Abbas in Iran, and then by road and rail through Baku to Moscow, St. Petersburg and beyond. In the longer term, the next route can be laid along the western coast of the Caspian Sea and along the new railway, which connects Kazakhstan, Turkmenistan and Iran. This route may well reduce the price and time required for transportation of goods between India and Russia.

It is expected that this route will become the engine of commerce in a vast region that is quickly integrated and more developed. The North-South Transport Corridor and other related projects will enable India to bypass Pakistan overland into the centre of the Eurasian continent. This is very attractive for India, especially if one considers that China is engaged in the realization of its China-Pakistan economic corridor.

India has also been politically active in the region. In 2018, India and Pakistan became full members of the Shanghai Cooperation Organization, which includes 4 Central Asian countries, Russia and China. In addition, India is also considering entering into a partnership with the Euro Asian Economic Union (EAEU), which includes the Russian Federation, the Republic of Belarus, Kazakhstan, Kyrgyzstan and Armenia. Nevertheless, the consequences of the efforts on the part of New Delhi, aimed at intensifying transport routes to Central Asia, go far beyond traditional geopolitics and more optimal transportation of their goods. At present, India is already ranked 4th among the largest consumers of electricity, and the demand for it in India is increasing quite rapidly, thus, the supply of natural resources is a critical component of relations with Central Asia.

India's Humanitarian Co-operation in Central Asia

India is in constructive dialogue on humanitarian issues with many stakeholders, including the countries of Central Asia, in which comprehensive diplomatic relations and humanitarian projects aimed at interaction and development will play a significant role. India is promoting its humanitarian projects in Central Asia primarily in the social sphere. India's Central Asia "Central Asia Connect Policy" strategy provides support for the construction of modern universities, hospitals, communications network and centres for the promotion of technological development. For example, the opening of a military hospital in 2014, which was built with the financial support of India, can be considered a positive interaction experience. The hospital is located in the Farkhor valley on the border of the Republic of Tajikistan and the Islamic Republic of Afghanistan. In the Republic of Uzbekistan, with the assistance of cultural and foreign policy structures of India, new ideological research centres have been opened and more than 350 agreements and memoranda on cooperation with research centres and universities of India have been published. (Letnyakov, D.E., 2017).

Often there are events aimed at disseminating cultural and scientific information about Indian achievements. With the financial assistance of India, the Centre for the Use of World Advances in Information and Communication Areas was opened at the University of Information Technology of Uzbekistan. Through internship programs, Uzbek citizens take courses in English and IT in India, and each year over 150 interns receive free training in the newest specialized institutions in New Delhi and other Indian cities.

Currently, under the aegis of Indian Council for Cultural Relations (ICCR), students of the Republic of Uzbekistan are offered training in various postgraduate, graduate and undergraduate programs at major universities in India. The Embassy of India in Uzbekistan and the Cultural Centre of India provide financial assistance in publishing Hindi textbooks for high schools, which is the first fundamental Hindi textbook in Uzbekistan. In 2018, Al-Farabi Kazakh National University hosted a presentation on the Hindi-Kazakh and a Kazakh-Hindi dictionary, which is the first of its kind in Kazakh.

In 2012, at the first "India-Central Asia", dialogue which was held in Bishkek, Deputy Foreign Minister Edapak Akhamed noted that India intended to open an Indo-Central Asian University in Bishkek with information technology, management and linguistics faculties. Currently, Indian students are enrolled in the medical faculties at the International University of Science and Business, Akhunbaeva Kyrgyz State Medical Academy and the International Higher School of Medicine at the International University of Kyrgyzstan. Thanks to such projects, India will be able to develop multilateral cooperation in the field of joint scientific research.

Central Asian states have a vested interest in the normalization of relations between India and Pakistan. The entry of India and Pakistan into the SCO imposes a number of obligations on them, including cooperation in the fight against terrorism, extremism and separatism. On January 14, 2019, there was a meeting of foreign ministers (including Afghanistan) at the India-Central Asia dialogue in Samarkand. It was attended by the foreign ministers of Uzbekistan: Abdulaziz Kamilov, India: Sushma Swaraj, Kazakhstan: Beibut Atamkulov, Kyrgyzstan: Chingiz Aydarbekov, Tajikistan: Sirojiddin Muhriddin, Turkmenistan: Rashid Meredov and Afghanistan: Salahuddin Rabbani (Ilyasov, A., 2017).

Following the meeting, the foreign ministers made a

statement indicating that they welcome the participation of Afghanistan in the first dialogue meeting as an important part of regional cooperation, and the transit of goods and energy. The participants expressed the support and commitment of their respective countries to peace, security and stability in Afghanistan, assistance in establishing the peace process, as well as promoting the economic reconstruction of Afghanistan through the implementation of joint projects.

The heads of the foreign affairs agencies noted the importance of sustainable economic growth in Afghanistan by attracting Afghan women to participate in public life. The potential for joint initiatives in cultural events and research projects with Afghanistan was also noted. The parties expressed their commitment to the development of bilateral and multilateral dynamic, productive, and friendly relations between India and Central Asia, and reaffirmed their desire for cooperation, mutual support, and joint solution of topical issues in order to ensure security, stability and sustainable development. They also condemned terrorism in all its forms and manifestations and agreed to cooperate in fight against terrorism, which is a threat to people and economies around the world.

The parties discussed the possibilities and areas of cooperation in the areas of mutual trade, bilateral investment, innovation, technology in key industries, energy, information technology, pharmaceuticals and agriculture, and education. They also confirmed their readiness to promote the development of direct business contacts, and cooperation among companies. The need to promote cooperation at the level of small and medium-sized businesses, start-ups, and venture business is significant.

The ministers drew attention to the need to expand and establish mutually beneficial economic and cultural ties between the regions and cities of India and Central Asia and expressed their intention to contribute to this direction. They accepted the invitation of Minister Sushma Swaraj to hold the next ministerial meeting in 2020 in India.

The meeting of the Foreign minister of Uzbekistan Abdulaziz Kamilov with Sushma Swaraj—as well as the first ministerial meeting of the dialogue India-Central Asia with the participation of Afghanistan—held in Samarkand symbolizes a shift in foreign policy strategy of New Delhi in Central Asia. India possesses an ability to assist in the peaceful restoration of the Afghan economy. New Delhi pledged to participate in the reconstruction of transport infrastructure and water supply, construction of housing and medical facilities, and taking custody of 116 projects in 31 provinces of Afghanistan.

In addition, India plans to build several new hydropower plants and solar power plants there. India, expanding its presence in Central Asia and Afghanistan, is directly competing with Beijing. True, with the positions that the Chinese side has already staked here, it has been quite difficult for New Delhi to compete with them. But they should start now even if it is late to the game, as the nodal points of the "Belt and Strip" initiative have not yet been connected. Today, India is working for the future in order to use the North-South international transport corridor to Europe, while rejecting the Chinese Belt and Path.

A significant obstacle to the development of Indian relations with the countries of Central Asia encompasses difficulty of access to raw materials and markets in the countries of the region. Pakistan blocks land transport links between India and Afghanistan, while China limits the possibility of establishing trade between India and the countries of Central Asia through Xinjiang. As a result, trade between India and the countries of Central Asia is predominantly carried out in a "roundabout way"—through the ports and transport network of Iran. Over the decade, the project of the trans-Afghan gas pipeline, whose financing is impossible without stabilizing the situation in Afghanistan, has not made any progress.

The growth of Indian political and economic influence in Central Asia has turned out to be low and insufficient to bolster Indian interests in the region. Although India, having strengthened political ties and military cooperation with Tajikistan, has gained an additional military-political advantage in its rivalry with Pakistan, yet New Delhi cannot compete with strengthening Chinese positions in Central Asia. At present, India needs to be considered not only from the point of view of its economic indicators, but also as a clear example of a dynamically developing economy, capable of making significant adjustments to the system of today's international relations.

Conclusion

In conclusion, it is to be noted that even today one may observe active propaganda and Indian soft power, India touts its projects such as the North-South Transport Corridor, which could be considered to be a new model for a new world order. Soft power in India is the formation of a model of the largest non Western type of democracy and the further development of promising integration in projects. In Central Asia, the Government of India is using the mechanisms of soft power quite well to carry out various humanitarian projects. However, it can be stated that India has not had a noticeable impact on the countries of the region yet. Nevertheless, India may well become one of the key players in Central Asia.

At the heart of India's real desire to develop policy in Central Asia lies in two fundamental factors. The first factor is related to energy, as India's need for energy resources is growing. The second factor is due to the geopolitical interests of India, lining up in the context of the Grand Strategy of Concentric Rings, called analyst Raja Mohana (2006), which is enclosed by circular orbits of Indian influence, first neighbouring countries, and then the distant countries.

References

Hymans, Jacques E.C. (2009), "India's Soft Power and Vulnerability", *India Review*, Vol. 8, No. 3, pp. 234-265.

Mohan, R. (2006), "India and the Balance of Power", *Foreign*

Affairs, Vol. 85, No. 4, pp. 17-32, available at: http://users.clas.ufl.edu/zselden/Course%20Readings/Mohan.pdf.

Nye, J. (1991), "Bound to Lead: The Changing Nature of American Power", Basic Books, New York.

Nye, J. (2004), "Soft Power: The Means to Success in World Politics", New York: Public Affairs.

Non-English

Ильясов А. Центральная Азияи Индияо бъединяту силиявбо рьбестерроризмом, 2017, Электронныйресурс, Режимдоступа: https://www.gazeta.uz/ru/2019/01/14/minister-meeting.

ЛетняковД.Э., ЕмельяноваН.Н. Стратегии «мягкойсилы» впостсоветской Центральной Азии: Россия, США, Китай, Индия, Журнал «МирРоссии», 2017, [Электронныйресурс]. – Режимдоступа: https://cyberleninka.ru/article/n/strategii-myagkoy-sily-v-postsovetskoy-tsentralnoy-azii-rossiya-vs-ssha-kitay-indiya.

Н. Минасян. Концепция «мягкойсилы» вконтекстетеор иймеждународныхотношений, 21-йвек, №3, 2017, [Электронныйресурс]. – Режимдоступа: http://www.noravank.am/rus/articles/detail.php?ELEMENT_ID=16242.

НарендраМоди. [Электронныйресурс], Режимдоступа: https://www.facebook.com/narendramodi/photos/a.10150164299700165/10161362388180165/?type=3&theater.

ПанфиловаВ. ИндияукрепляетсявЦентральнойАзии, 2019, [Электронныйресурс], Режимдоступа: http://inozpress.kg/news/view/id/53723.

Шепард, У. Осторожно, Китай! ИндиясоздаетсвойсобственныйШелковыйпуть, Изд, Россиясегодня, 2017, [Электронныйресурс], Режимдоступа: https://inosmi.ru/politic/20170701/239710839.html.

4

Varied Paradigms, Co-ordination and Co-operation between the Two Regions

Meha Pant

Introduction

The regions of Central Asia and India share a historical relationship which incorporates the political, economic and cultural dimensions in a defined proportion. With the stagnation in the relations between them during the Soviet rule and a later realization of the significance of Central Asia to India, all seems to be working in the right direction for the two regions. The regions seem to be cooperating with each other well on the economic front with the recent unveiling of the TAPI gas pipeline, yet there remain some dimensions which though common still remain unexplored to a large extent. This is the dimension of linkage between terrorism with ethnicity and religion and both have had a major impact on the politics of both sides. India and Central Asia on separate fronts have faced the common enemy of terrorism which has not only hampered development but has also escalated the role of organized criminal groups on the social front.

Thus, the purpose of this paper is to highlight the linkage in terms of a common enemy where the application of secondary sources will be incorporated. In this globalized world, where geographical barriers stand diluted to such an extent that ignorance of the vitality of the subject stands a reason for providing an impetus to such transnational organized criminal organizations.

The Indian subcontinent and Central Asia have had shared historical, economic, political and cultural relations with each other since times immemorial, except for a temporary setback in relations during the Soviet era. When looked at from the perspective of geographical association between the two, the notion of 'Greater Central Asia' comes into play. In accordance with this concept, the region of 'Greater Central Asia' is an amalgamation of the five Central Asian States, Afghanistan and Turkic Xingjian (region of China) extending to the northern parts of Pakistan, Khorasan Province of Iran, Tataristan in Russia and even North India (Joshi, 2011).

In contemporary times, the two regions seem to be adopting a cooperative approach. What needs to be taken into consideration in this cooperation between the two regions is the advent of transnational organized crime and international terrorism. These two issues have equally been responsible for havoc between the two and thus exists a high priority for a viable solution to the problem. The recent TAPI gas pipeline initiative, is a mark of cooperation on the economic and political front between the two regions, which must be kept under surveillance due to threats from various terrorist groups active in Central Asia. History, culture, economics and political issues have played a major role in the defining of the relationship between the two regions hence a deeper understanding of the same is extremely important to understand the contemporary politics between the two regions.

Historical Linkages

The two regions have been linked to each other since times immemorial. Until the sea route from Europe to India was not discovered till 15th century AD, Central Asia served as a transmitter of trade, knowledge and invaders to the Indian subcontinent. A viable journey was fore taken for the profits it rendered to the traders and the empires connected to the route. The two regions have shared immense history with the rulers of the Indian-subcontinent like the Kushans, Babur and Tamerlane having their origins in Central Asia. Islam, the second largest religion in India was introduced by these Central Asian civilization heads. However, the religion of

Buddhism with its origin in India has had a major impact on Central Asia and is still widely practiced in the region (Joshi, 2011).

A mutual relation in the cultural and historical term has been well shared as part of the engagements between India and Central Asia. The two regions seem to complement each other with clear evidence of transactions both political and cultural. The relations between the two regions date back to the Palaeolithic age. The Pamiri and Hindukush culture seem to link the Indian Kangra Valley and the Gissan Culture of Central Asia, a part of the Sohan culture which was also the most prominent of the Palaeolithic cultures (Kumar, 2007). Niranjan M. Khilnani stated that, "in the ancient and medieval period there was a great process of mutual cultural enrichment between India and Central Asia" (Ahmar, 1984). The link between the two regions has been immense and has resulted in the upsurge of various theories in regard to the affinity between the two regions.

The Aryan Theory

The "Aryan Theory" has derived the Aryans coming to India from Central Asia as a result of the various nomadic waves which arose from the region during various times. In his writing, Bal has clearly mentioned the Aryans originating from Central Asia (Bal, 2004) and arriving in the Indian subcontinent. He states that the Aryans brought in their culture and language with them as a result of which much similarity can be found between the Indian subcontinent and the Central Asian states. Historian T. Srinov in his study stated that around the 3rd and 4th century BC (Srinov, 2000), around the post-Vedic period, there was a deeper intermingling between the two regions. He further states that there is a mention of Central Asian warriors (Saka, Pahlava, Persians), Kambojas (Galcha Speaking people of Tajikistan), Rishek (Yueh-Chi or Kushanas), (Chena, Huna and Yavana) being invited in the epic battle of both Ramayana and Mahabharata (Gupta, 2002).

Harappan Civilization and the Two Regions

The Harappan civilization and the excavations within have provided much proof in regard to the connection between the two. Ahmad in his work "India and its Role in the New Central Asia", has stated that the Harappan civilization ruins have camels and horses which are a clear indication of the caravans and linkages between the two regions. Apart from the Harappan civilization, there are ample of places in the Central Asian region which provide evidence of the interaction of the two regions. The "Excavation of Tak-Mak region of Kyrgyzstan, Amu Darya Valley in Southern Uzbekistan, North-East of Samarkand in Uzbekistan, many places in Turkmenistan and Kazakhstan, provide ample evidence of Indo -Central Asian links from ancient times" (Kumar, 2007). Also, places like Kara Tepa, Isykata, Kranayerzka, AK Beshin, Yer Kurgan, Dalvergin Tepa, and Fayaz Tepa are evidence of the mutual fellowship between the two regions.

Central Asia became a point of infusion between various dynasties, kingdoms and empires (Lockard, 2010) like that between the Greeks and the Indians (Rowland, 1989). Central Asian region has always been termed as the transmitter of culture, history, trade, economies and dynasties due to it being an important part of the Silk Route which joined East with West.

The Greeks

The Greeks are said to have inculcated values among the Central Asians in terms of the Indian culture with the introduction of the region to Indian practices of worshipping Indian Gods and Goddesses (Liu, 2011). Greeks rather played the part of creating a fusion in the cultural practices between the two regions.

The Mauryan Empire

Mauryan Empire (Lockard, 2014) had been a primary source of interaction between the two regions which apart from the conquests and economic affiliations, played an important part in the spread of Buddhism in the region. The two rulers Bindusara and Ashoka were the most prominent propagators of the religion in Central Asia.

The Kushan Dynasty

The culture and traditions of the western part of India has been much influenced by the Saka rulers who originated from the region of Central Asia (Agnew, 1997). Apart from the Saka's, the Kushan Dynasty has had a great impact on the culture of Central Asia which is prominent in the Buddhist part found in the region, especially the Gandhara school of art. Kashmir and Gandhara were the interaction point of Buddhism within the region of Central Asia as it was through this region that the Central Asians were introduced to the teachings of Buddhism.

The Mongols and the Turks

The Mongols and the Turks have been the prominent invaders from Central Asia who changed the whole equation of the Central Asian-Indian equation. The Turk scholars in various fields had worked under various emperors of India and were well accustomed with the nature and wealth of the Indian subcontinent. The Turks arrived in India in the 11th century with the motive to plunder wealth and propagate Islam in the Indian subcontinent (Liu, 2011).

The Mongols on the other hand came to the Indian subcontinent in the 13th century and contributed immensely to the present state of Indian culture in terms of propagation of languages like Guru, Mani, and Ratna and also the religion of Sufism. The region of Kashmir which had earlier been a point of propagation of Buddhism into the Central Asian region now became a receiving point to that of Sufism. The commonality here was that both Sufism and Buddhism propagate peace and religious tolerance (Singh, 2015).

The Mughals

The last and the most impactful empires to come to India

was the Mughal Empire—invaders who came to India to loot but gave India a rich history to be savoured for generations. The Mughal Empire (Foltz, 1998) was the longest rule of a Central Asian force in India as they came during the 16th century and ruled until 1857 to be ousted by the British. Their kingdom ranged from the cities of Delhi, Lahore, Agra and Fatehpur Sikri to that of the Central Asian towns Samarqand, Bukhara, Khorasan, and Balkh (Shodhganga).

The relationship between the two regions has been of give and take where both have impacted each other in various dimensions. Kharoshti, an Indian language, was widely used for documentation purposes in Central Asia, especially the Eastern part near to India, while Sanskrit and Brahmi have been popular as part of literature, culture and study of astronomy and medicine (Banerjee, 1994). There are also events of exchange of students of various arts between the two regions which is very similar to the contemporary exchange of students between the two regions majorly for educational purposes (Shodhganga). The mutual transaction between the two regions has been established since the prehistoric times and continues till the contemporary times (Researchgate, 2015).

Economic Links

The Mughal Khans of India long dreamt of making Central Asia a part of their empire, yet the fact that it did not happen, did not affect trade between the two regions for long (Gopal, 2001). There is mention of a city of Indians located north of the Amu Darya which later also became a transit point of Indian medical and scientific knowledge between India the Middle East and Europe. India was known for its woollen cloth, turbans, white cotton cloth, chintz, molasses, sugar, turmeric, pepper and books of "mohammedan" (Islamic) culture on theology and law (Izzut-oolah,1872) in Central Asia, while the Central Asian states exported silk to the Indian Subcontinent (Klemm, 1888). "Russian boxes called sunduks with metal work were quite popular along with tea pots and cups in bright colours and samovars in the north-western region of India" (Andreyeyev, 1908). Despite Indian goods enjoying a good market in Central Asian households, indigo was the most prominent import from India to Central Asia (Nebolsin, 1855).

Trade Routes and Centres of Trade

With trade between the two regions at its zenith, there were a number of trade routes and centres which played an important role in the entire process. There were a number of cities which remained focal points of the entire trade process like that of Lahore, Kabul, Multan, Kandhar, Bukhara, Samarkand, Khiva and Merv, Peshawar and Shikarpur.

Apart from trade centres, there were a number of trade routes which existed at that time contributing to the entire trade process. There were three major trade routes between the two regions which were prevalent during the times of the Mughals. The threc major trade routes during the time were as follows. The first trade route ranged from Lahore-Peshawar-Khyber Pass-Kabul-Bamian-TashKurgan-Mazar-i-Sharif-Amu River-Bukharan Khanate-Karshi-Bukhara (Gopal, 2001). The second trade route started from Karachi-Indus-Shikarpur-Bolan Pass-Kandhar-Heart-Mashad (Persia) to end in Ashkhabad (Gopal, 2001). The third route was from India through Herat to Merv (Gopal, 2001).

Escalation of the rivalry between the British and the Russian rulers in the year 1881 put an end to any legal trade between the two regions leading to a dip of 15-20 percent in trade (Babakhodzhaev, 1965). This led to the diversion of trade between India and Central Asia through a different route of Ferghana-Kashgar-Kashmir. The conflict had an adverse impact on trade in the region leading to a change in the preference of the people, as a new market of cheaper Russian goods was established compared to expensive British goods by the end of the 19th century (Gubarevich, 1912).

The intensification of strife led to a large decline in economic transactions between the two regions which led to initiatives by various leaders to boost the economy of their respective countries. Moorcroft in his book mentions a letter written by the foreign minister in Russia, Count Nesselrode, where the Russian Emperor desired the opening up of the gates of friendly intercourse which would lead to the clearing of the road of traffic between the merchants of Russia and Punjab from all impediments" (Moorcroft, 1821). Even in the Anglo-Russian Convention of 1907, a demand was raised to link India and Central Asia by rail which the Russian press of Central Asia termed as a realization of the dreams of Peter the great" (Turkestanskii, 1908). These dreams were never realized as the angst due to the Anglo-Rus rivalry did not abate and the rise of a communist Russia only worsened relations between the two.

Political Linkages

Central Asia has been a transmitter of heritage, economics, knowledge and, unfortunately, turmoil. Central Asian invaders like Babar, Tamerlane, and the Kushans have been able to establish rule over the Indian subcontinent and it was only after the advent of the British Empire that relations between the two regions came to a standstill. British fear of Russian conquest reaching the folds of the Indian subcontinent later led to the Anglo-Russian wars. Yet, even during the Indian freedom struggle, political relations continued with Russia through communist insurgents who continuously sought Soviet help in this matter.

Role of the Soviets in the Escalation of Feuds

The disregard of ethnic, tribal, linguistic and geographical factors in the demarcation of borders during the Cold War led to many problems in governance, cross-border regulations, heightened security concerns and interstate disputes post-Soviet collapse (Sehgal, 2011). This led to an upsurge of informal networks of power, which were based on clan, interest and region. The absorption of Central Asian states into the folds of the Soviet Union led to a state ban on religion; there were many clashes in the name of religion, however these were silenced by the authorities. An impetus to the feeling occurred from 1979-1989. The Anglo-Russian rivalry had now taken the form of the Afghan war.

Many Central Asians be it Tajiks, Uzbeks, Krygyz, Kazakhs or Turks, were sent as Soviet soldiers to fight in Afghanistan. This is when these soldiers came in contact with their counterparts to realize the affiliation whether religious or cultural that they all shared. As a result, there was smuggling of the Holy Quran into the Central Asian states, something which had been curbed for decades. The events led to the peaceful Central Asian states adopting an extremist approach as the Afghani nationals had always been adherents of Wahhabi or violent form of Islam (Knysh, A., 2004), (Ayoob, M., 2004).

The war shifted from fighting aggressors to fighting godless communists leading to a clash of civilizations of Islam and Christianity in the wake of the Afghan independence struggle. At this time, Pakistan became a frontline state as an initiator of Islam and supplier of arms against the *kafirs* on the Afghan front. Yet, while one war was for emancipation and freedom, there began another war of drug trafficking which would have adverse consequences in the future.

Post-1991 Indo-Central Asia Relations

An amalgamation of the changes under Soviet rule resulted in a struggle for prominence amongst the Central Asian states as they struggled for prominence in the midst of independence (Sehgal, 2011). With this scenario at the wake of Central Asian independence and the end of the Cold War, relations between Central Asia and India did not receive an immediate impetus as both regions were busy dealing with more pressing issues. As the Central Asian states after having attained independence were in search of a definite direction both culturally and politically, the Indian state was engrossed in fighting the impact of Cold War disintegration and also welcoming the new air of development with GPL.

The Central Asian states while asserting their sovereignty wanted to move away from the Russian 'Bear Hug' while inclining towards US and Western powers for their security and economic issues (Sehgal, 2011). The prevalence of NATO, western powers, Pakistan and other Islamic states in the region has been used by the Central Asian republics as an opportunity of Islamization, modernization and improvement of their armed forces in order to combat the regional challenges of drug trafficking, religious extremism, terrorism and proliferation of weapons of mass destruction (Sehgal, 2011). Yet, the Central Asian approach towards the state of India has been one of a friendly neighbour which has no selfish and evil intentions in the area.

The coming up of the government in 2014 under the leadership of Prime Minister Narendra Modi has initiated a fresh round of bonding between the two regions. In 2015, the Indian Prime Minister paid a visit to the Central Asian states. This visit was much beyond the Afghan factor and more about the revival of the relations between the two. This visit resurfaced the region to that of prominence in terms of Indian foreign policy and has been termed as a "Golden Era" of India-Central Asia relationship.

The Indian Initiative

The first initiative from the Republic of India towards the Central Asian states was the 1995 visit of late Prime Minister P.V. Narsimha Rao to Turkmenistan. During this visit, while highlighting Indian motives in Central Asia he stated, "we are independent partners with no selfish motives. We only desire an honest and open friendship and to promote stability and cooperation without causing harm to a third country".

This visit led to the establishment of ties between the two states which were based on geographies of energy, religion, ethnic and tribal divisions (Sehgal, 2011). In terms of defence relationship between the two, the focus was on sharing intelligence, training, and servicing and upgrading military hardware. India has since proven itself to be a cooperative and friendly power which not only helps the Central Asian states with aid but also shares a common enemy (Sehgal, 2011).

In the contemporary times, the policies of the Modi government to renew relations with these countries have led to an increased cooperation between the two regions. After assuming office as the Prime Minister of India in 2014, Mr. Narendra Modi pledged to revive India's relations with the rest of the world with the acknowledgement of India's as a rising regional and world power.

In 2015, Prime Minister Modi paid a visit to the Central Asian states. Gifts for each Central Asian leader had been carefully crafted and foreign policy finely sown. This visit came at the right time when both Russia and China have increased their presence in the region. These two states share borders with the region unlike India which has no direct connectivity. While the meeting with the countries of Uzbekistan, Kyrgyzstan and Tajikistan revolved around the topics of boosting trade and connectivity, the talks with the countries of Kazakhstan and Turkmenistan was more about energy cooperation between the two regions (Pant, 2015).

The 2015 Modi's visit was vital as various development planks on the international and regional level were taking place including: (a) Russia's renewed assertion in Central Asia following its standoff with the West over Ukraine; (b) China's fresh push for building connectivity infrastructure to link China with Europe via Central Asia under its Silk Road Economic Belt initiative; (c) the prospects of Iran coming to the regional fore following its recent nuclear breakthrough with the major powers; and, (d) the emerging situation in Afghanistan in the context of growing Afghanistan-Pakistan proximity to rehabilitate the Taliban (P. Stobdan, 2015).

In 2018, a uranium deal was signed between the countries of Kazakhstan and India along with defence cooperation and railway line agreements (Economic Times, 2018). In June 2019, Prime Minister Narendra Modi again met the Central Asian leaders during the SCO summit. PM Modi, in a statement before his visit to Bishkek from June 13-14, said, "The Summit is expected to discuss the global security situation, multilateral economic cooperation, people-to-people exchanges and topical issues of international and regional importance. On the sidelines of the Summit, I also plan to meet several leaders bilaterally" (India Today, 2019).

In the contemporary times, the relations between the two states have been treading towards a formative journey which is a positive take on the foreign policy relationship between the two regions.

Contemporary Issues and Indo-Central Asia Relations

India and Central Asia relationship is based on the ideal of becoming more open and progressive societies in terms of democratic and secularist nations while sharing common views on terrorism and drug trafficking.

What plays to the advantage of India and Central Asia relations also poses a danger for the same. The first point to be noted here is the proximity between India and Central Asian states. The two regions share two unstable neighbours, Pakistan and Afghanistan, which are considered to be the genesis point and also safe havens for illicit activities and non-traditional threats that pose a danger to these regions (Joshi, 2015).

Apart from trade, education, health, technology, and transport, the non-traditional threats have become a major issue between India and Central Asia. The two regions share certain points of concern which are common to both regions. It is these points which has led to the establishment of a more cooperative and coordinated relationship between the two areas.

Porosity of Borders: Both the regions of Central Asia and India share a common problem in regard to the porosity of their borders and also the infiltration of illicit traffic across the same. The porosity of the Central Asian borders, along with the vacuum created as a result of the sudden independence they attained, led to an increase in organized crime and other non-traditional threats like arms trafficking, narco trafficking, and extremism in the region. With regards to India, the existence of Pakistan has led to the borders of the state being constantly used to infiltrate illegal activities into the Indian subcontinent, be it terrorism or drugs.

Ideological Struggle and Terrorist Acts: Researchers opine that rather than being about extremism, it is more about an ideological struggle (Joshi, 2015), where rather than democratic and secular values, it is the extreme version of religion which is paid importance to. The Federally Administered Tribal Areas of Pakistan and Gorno-Badakshan on the north of Afghanistan have become new safe havens for these illicit forces. If seen from the perspective of development and peace, the involvement of these regions in these activities is one blame not be taken alone, but also by the administrative machinery of the respective governments. Both these areas have been ridiculed and shunned by the governments with no proper facilities to reach out to these areas.

This, as a result, leads to widespread poverty, hunger, and unemployment, along with inadequate knowledge of the real aspects of religion. These versions define the flow of people into terrorism and other activities as they become a means of earning the basic needs of life.

Drug Trafficking: India and Central Asia have recently come together to fight the problem of drug trafficking prevalent in both the regions. Drug trafficking from the region of Central Asia goes north and south which has become a big issue, especially after it got involved in the Golden Crescent which is a hub of drug production and marketing. Drug trafficking has not only made an impact on the market but also in the areas of transition. One result of this is the extensive abuse of drugs in Central Asian states. President Nursultan

Nazarbayev had once stated that in Kazakhstan, there are around 45,505 people including 1,927 adolescents and 4,420 women who have been registered with drug abuse (Joshi, 2015).

The country of Tajikistan has been termed as an "economy of drugs" by researchers, all initiatives and developments in the region are the result of money generated through drug trafficking in the region. The importance of this country in drug trafficking may be understood by the title it has earned as the bottleneck of drugs to Central Asia, clearly estimating it as the passage of afghan drugs to Central Asia through which they are further sent to the countries of Russia and Europe.

In regard to India, the Pakistan border serves as the biggest traffic point of drugs into India. There are various traffic points across the long border which these two countries share. The recent movie "*Udta Punjab*" had aptly portrayed the ongoing trade and its repercussions in India. Each year, numerous cases are identified in India and there has been a growth in rehabilitation camps across the country to fight the situation.

Pakistan and Afghanistan and Troubles Within: The Pakistani and the Afghani governments have also been unable to recover a large number of weapons which were left after the withdrawal of Soviet forces from Afghanistan. These weapons are both of Soviet origin and those which Pakistan supplied for fighting the Soviets. The weapons once used for attainment of independence are being used to kill its own people while spreading a violent form of Islam which was never a forte of the Central Asian states. With regards to India, the very spurts of threats emanating from Afghanistan have fostered nuances of the same in the Indian subcontinent with the focal point being Kashmir. The state funded terrorism of Pakistan with, safe havens in Afghanistan, the drug trafficking through the borders of India, and weapons smuggling has had a similar impact on the stability of the nation.

Co-operation against Non-traditional Threats: Central Asia and India, understanding their mutual interests and the prevalence of non-traditional threats have signed many agreements for cooperation in the field. With the recent Pulwama attack in India, the pressure on Pakistan has mounted at the world level and also for initiation of talks with the Afghan Taliban for bringing instability in Central Asia. In a recent meeting between the leaders of Afghanistan, Central Asia and India in January 2019, the statement issued at the end by the leaders stated, "All sides condemn terrorism in all its forms and manifestations and have agreed to cooperate in countering terrorism which poses a threat to the people and economies of the world" while further stating that "we have reaffirmed our willingness for cooperation, mutual support, and joint solutions on relevant issues in order to ensure security, stability and sustainable development in the region", (Economic Times, 2019).

Conclusion

Contemporary relations between Central Asia and India have been based on years of historical, economic and cultural ties. Recently, non-traditional security threats have secured a much talked about position between the regions, which serves as a reason for heightened cooperation and coordination between the two. The growing awareness about the non-traditional issues has led to increased cooperation between the two states which have also led to the revival of other sectors as well. The 2015 visit of Modi to the Central Asian states gave a boost to relations between the regions. Since then, the two regions of Central Asia and India stand in coordination with each other for the journey ahead.

References

Agnew, N. (ed.), (1997), "Conservation of Ancient Sites on the Silk Road", proceedings of the International Conference on the Conservation of Grotto Sites' Getty Publications.

Ahmar, Moonis (1992), "India and its Role in the New Central Asia", *Pakistan Horizon*, Vol. 45, No. 3, July, p. 59, from Khilnani, Niranjan M., 'Realities of Indian Foreign Policy', New

Delhi: ABC Publishing House, 1984, pp. 167-168.

Ahmar, Moonis (1992), "India and its Role in the New Central Asia", *Pakistan Horizon*, Vol. 45, No. 3, July, p. 59, from Khilnani, Niranjan M., 'Realities of Indian Foreign Policy', New Delhi: ABC Publishing House, 1984, p. 53.

Ayoob, M. (2004), "Political Islam: Image and Reality", *World Policy Journal,* 21(3), pp. 1-14, available at: http://www.jstor.org/stable/40210231.

Babakhodzhaev, M.A. (1965), "Russko-Afghan Skietorgo Voekono Micheskiesviazi", pp. 49-50,Tashkent.

Bal, Suryakant Nijanand (2004), "Central Asia: A Strategy for India's Look-North Policy", New Delhi: Lancer Publishers and Distributors.

Economic Times (2015), available at: https://economictimes.indiatimes.com/news/defence/pm-modis-visit-to-central-asia-india-and-kazakhstan-ink-deals-on-uranium-supply-defence/articleshow/47996585.cms?from=mdr.

Foltz, R. (1998), "Mughal India and Central Asia", Oxford University Press, USA.

Gopal, S. (2001), "The Economic Relations between India and Central Asia in the 19th Century", in Gopal Surendra (ed.), 'India and Central Asia: Cultural, Economic and Political Links', pp. 45-60, Delhi: Shipra Publications.

Gubarevich, A.F. (1912), "Znachemie Turkestana v torgovleRossii S Sopredel'nymiSranamiAzii", in "Materia lydlyaizucheniyaKhlopKorodstva", vyp, II, (131), St. Petersburg.

Gupta, S.P. (2002), "Hindu Gods in Western Central Asia: A Lesser Known Chapter of Indian History", *Dialogue,* April-June, 3(2), pp. 142-143.

India Today (2019), available at: https://www.indiatoday.in/india/story/pm-modi-extends-central-asian-outreach-to-hold-bilateral-talks-with-kyrgyzstan-during-sco-summit-1547716-2019-06-13.

Joshi, N. (2011), "Reconnecting India and Central Asia: Emerging Security Dimensions", New Delhi: Pentagon Press.

Joshi, N. (2015), "Indian and Central Asian Perspectives on Regional Security", in Bhatia, R. and Anusseitova, M. (ed.), 'India and Central Asia: Exploring New Horizon for Cooperation', 60-85, Almaty: Institute of Oriental Studies.

Knysh, A. (2004), "A Clear and Present Danger: 'Wahhabism' as a Rhetorical Foil", *Die Welt DesIslams,* 44(1), new series, pp. 3-26, available at: http://www.jstor.org/stable/1571334.

Kumar, B.B. (2007), "India and Central Asia: Links and Interactions", in Roy, J.N. and Kumar, B.B. (eds.), "Classical to Contemporary Periods", Delhi: Astha Bharti Publishers, p. 4.

Lockard, C.A. (2010), "The Sea Common to All: Maritime Frontiers, Port Cities, and Chinese Traders in the Southeast Asian Age of Commerce", *Journal of World History*, pp. 219-247.

Lockard, C.A. (2014), "Societies, Networks, and Transitions: Since 1450: A Global History", Cengage Learning.

Liu, M.Y. (2011), "Central Asia in the Post-Cold War World", *Annual Review of Anthropology*, 40.

Nebolsin, P. (1855), "OcherkiTorgovliRossii So SredneiAzii-Zapiski Imp. RusskogogeograficheskogoObshchestva, Kn.X, p. 313.

Pant (2015), available at: https://www.orfonline.org/research/pm-modis-well-timed-visit-to-central-asia.

Research Gate (2015), available at: https://www.researchgate.net/publication/278403637_India_and_Central_Asia_An_Interpretation_of_Mutually_Indelible_Historical_Relationship_and_its_Multi_Faceted_Impact.

Rowland, R.H. (1989), "National and Regional Population Trends in the USSR, 1979--89: Preliminary Results from the 1989 Census", *Soviet Geography*, 30(9), pp. 635-669.

Roychoudhury, S., Roy, S., Basu, A., Banerjee, R., Vishwanathan, H., Rani, M.U. and Majumder, P.P. (2001), "Genomic Structures and Population Histories of Linguistically Distinct Tribal Groups of India", *Human Genetics*, 109(3), pp. 339-350.

Sehgal, Anand V. (2011), "Strategic Environment in the Central Asia and India", in Joshi, N. (ed.), 'Reconnecting India and Central Asia: Emerging Security Dimensions', 20-40, New Delhi: Pentagon Press.

Shodhganga, available at: https://shodhganga.inflibnet.ac.in/bitstream/10603/204454/8/08_chapter%201.pdf.

Srinov, T. (2000), "India and Central Asia in Pre-Islamic Period", paper presented in a seminar, Contact between Central Asia and the Indian Subcontinent in the Second Millennium BC, June 12-

13, Tashkent, Uzbekistan.

Stobdan, P. (2015), available at: https://idsa.in/issuebrief/TheModifactorinCentralAsia_pstobdan_240714.

TurkestanskiiKurier (1908), "TurkestanskiiSbornik", T, 458, 190, No. 65, p. 149.

5

India and Central Asian Countries: Moving Towards Each Other

Erkin Baydarov

Introduction

A multi-faceted foreign policy of the Central Asian republics (with the exception of Turkmenistan) has contributed to the establishment of cooperation with various global and regional actors including India. India has long-standing friendly ties with the countries of Central Asia. The new independent states of the region established diplomatic relations with "the country of a thousand religions" due to geographical and cultural-historical proximity of Central Asia to India (Hesse, 2000), which has revived and given new impetus to the development of relations. In the past, China provided most of the development funding for Central Asia, while interaction with India, had been limited to technological exchange (Baydarov, 2018; Savkovich, 2012). Since the entry of India into the Shanghai Cooperation Organization (SCO), the region has focused more attention on India and South Asia as a whole.

India's membership of the SCO provides New Delhi with new opportunities to expand its interests in the region. India regards Central Asian countries not only as natural partners in cooperation in the field of politics and security, but as partners in trade and economic sphere also. Moreover, resource-rich Central Asia, through which a significant part of the infrastructure of the Chinese Belt and Road Initiative passes, garners a great deal of attention from China and India.

If Beijing, implementing its "One Belt, One Road"

initiative, is trying to maximize utilization of the region's vast reserves of minerals and hydrocarbons, as well as expand the presence of its products in its markets, New Delhi is also trying to activate its Central Asian program, though the lack of a direct connection with the region is a significant obstacle (Yerekesheva, 2017; Troitsky, 2013).

The Indian establishment is also being pushed to pursue a more active policy in Central Asia by concerns about the steady growth of China's military-industrial-economic complex. At the same time, with a growing economy and increasing energy needs, it is vital for India to seek new sources of hydrocarbons. In addition to bilateral opportunities for cooperation, India has some tools to increase its influence in the Central Asian region. In particular, cooperation within the framework of the SCO provides India with the opportunity to become a part of the process of regional cooperation (Orakbaeva, 2017).

Connect Central Asia Policy

The collapse of the USSR in the 1990s marked the beginning of a new global geopolitical configuration. India's internal economic reforms during this period enabled them to formulate a new geo-strategic concept of the "Extended Neighbourhood". This concept, based on historical and cultural traditions and considering the region of Central Asia as a neighbouring region and a natural partner, is intended to improve Indian relations with the new independent states of Central Asia. The revitalization of India's policies in the region is due to its close proximity to Afghanistan and the presence of potential security threats that may spread in the region.

The "Connect Central Asia Policy" was announced in June 2012 in Bishkek by Edapakat Ahmed, the Deputy Minister of Foreign Affairs of the Republic of India, during the First India-Central Asia Dialogue. The main message of this program is that India views Central Asia through the prism of politics, which requires active participation in political and economic reality—for example, increased contacts between individuals and collectively between the parties is invaluable (Kaushiki, 2013: 84; Bisaria, 2013).

For India, the development of relations with the countries of Central Asia is associated with the need for them to solve their own political, strategic, and economic issues, such as peace and stability in an "expanded neighbourhood", joint coordination in fight against terrorism and solution of the problem of Afghanistan; strengthening of energy security, and rebuilding the Afghan economic situation. Moreover, realizing the necessity of Central Asia to solve their own economic, educational, transport, infrastructure, and security issues, India has found a niche at the intersection of mutually beneficial interests, resulting in the "Connect Central Asia Policy" programme.

India-Central Asia Development Prospects

India has had a changing role in the modern global economy in recent years. The average economic growth rate from 2013-2016 averaged 7.1 percent, which is above the world average of 2.5 percent over the same period, and higher than the 4 percent average in developing countries. If we consider the average annual contribution of India to the growth of the global economy in 2013-2016, then the country is among the main leaders contributing to 8.1 percent of the world economic growth and being one of the engines of growth of the world economy (Baidarov, 2018).

India, as the world's largest rapidly developing economy, needs to be considered not only in terms of its economic indicators, but also as an example of a dynamically developing economy capable of making substantial improvements to the current system of international development. The economic success of India in recent years has naturally changed the nature of its relations with Central Asia and brought them to a new level. In this regard, India is extremely interested in economic cooperation with Central Asia. However, New Delhi is well aware that the measures proposed for the realization of her aspirations are often delayed. That is why India chooses those areas in which it is the "strongest", as well as those which can give definite results in the medium term.

In the early 2000, India had big plans to participate in the development of Central Asia, a large number of Memorandums on Cooperation (MoCs) in the energy sector have been signed with Kazakhstan, Turkmenistan and Uzbekistan. But most of the MoCs failed to be implemented previously due to many factors, including connectivity. However, cooperation with Turkmenistan on gas supplies and investments in some infrastructure projects in Tajikistan got success to a great extent. As a result, India is not even among the ten largest investors in the energy sector of the region.

Taking into account Russian and Western penetration of the region, and the rapid growth in China in the regional energy sector, India is trying to find its niche. Even so, there are ample opportunities for cooperation between India and Central Asia in the field of both traditional and new forms of energy viz., hydrocarbons, hydropower, resources of the Caspian Sea, nuclear energy, TAPI and CASA 1000 projects, as well as technology for using renewable energy sources (Orakbaeva, 2017). India has only managed to penetrate Central Asian markets with pharmaceuticals. Up to 30 percent of Central Asian pharmaceutical products are imported from India. There has also been some uranium trade with Kazakhstan and Uzbekistan, and cotton trade with Uzbekistan.

In general, we can note the following priority areas in which India is ready to cooperate with the countries of Central Asia:

- Energy, mineral resources, agriculture (the cultivation and production of high value-added products, as well as their processing);
- Medicine—India seeks to go beyond purely pharmaceuticals and undertake the work for civilian hospitals/clinics;

- Educational development system;
- A digital network in the field of tele-medicine with a hub in India, which would unite all the countries of Central Asia;
- Construction, including medium-sized rolling steel plants;
- Transport routes and logistics. Particularly relevant for India is the intensive care unit of the North-South Transport Corridor; and
- The banking sector, which requires development, especially if tasks are to be set for the development of trade and economic relations. This is very important, given that India has signed agreements on strategic partnership with Kazakhstan, Uzbekistan and Tajikistan (Yerekesheva, 2017; Baydarov, 2018).

The development of trade and economic relations which remain at a low level, have not matched political rhetoric. India's trade with all the countries of Central Asia, only recently reached U$$ 1 billion. But now the situation is changing. According to the results of 2018, trade between Kazakhstan and India alone amounted to US$ 1.2 billion, displaying an annual increase of 26.5 percent. The entry of the country into the SCO is largely responsible for these increases due to innovation and investment (The Economic Times, 2019).

As a consequence, Kazakhstan is negotiating a free trade zone with India and is interested in discussing further expansion and deepening of trade, economic and investment ties. India, in turn, is considering the possibility of creating an air cargo hub in Kazakhstan. In addition, an Indian company, Oil and Natural Gas Corporation Limited (ONGC) is interested in buying a relatively large Kazakh oil company. As trade with India increases, however, exports from India to Central Asia are not keeping pace. For example, in 2018, exports from Kazakhstan to India increased by 30.1 percent and amounted to US$ 954.1 million. The main components included oil (US$ 741.6 million, +19.8 percent), chemical radioactive elements and their compounds (US$ 90.3 million, +15.3 percent) and silver in powder form (US$ 67.6 million). Conversely, imports of Indian products were extremely low. The main goods imported included medicines (US$ 66.6 million, +13 percent), flavoured tea (US$ 32.6 million, - 21.2 percent) and telephones (US$ 11.1 million, an increase of 64.4 times over the year) [MEA, India, 2016].

Although India has close and warm relations with all the Central Asian states, India's key Central Asian partners are undoubtedly Uzbekistan and Kazakhstan and they play a large role in strengthening New Delhi's position in the region. Tashkent is secretly viewed as the "backbone" of Central Asia, and occupies a high place in the regional policy of New Delhi. Uzbekistan, located in the heart of Central Asia, also plays a key role in maintaining peace, security and stability throughout the region of Central Asia, and is a significant force in global counterterrorism (Stobdan, P., 2015). The visits of the Uzbek President Shavkat Mirziyoyev to India indicate Uzbek reciprocation.

Afghanistan in the Foreign Policy of India and Central Asian Countries

Terrorism in Afghanistan and Pakistan is of great concern for both the Indian and Central Asian governments. The situation in Afghanistan remains bleak. Only a reduction of the military presence and a full economic recovery will reduce the level of potential internal conflict in Afghanistan. Therefore, the countries of Central Asia are hopeful that India will assist in this task. The top priority should be to provide targeted economic assistance to Afghanistan. In this regard, India's role is of great importance for the entire region. It should be noted that the two leading countries of the region—Kazakhstan and Uzbekistan—have their own programs of assistance to Afghanistan. Since the mid-2000s, Astana and Tashkent have cooperated in the areas of infrastructure, mining, and education. India has long supported the government of

Afghanistan and is involved in the reconstruction process in Afghanistan and is also inclined in favour of a peaceful resolution to the Afghan issue and removal of extremists and terrorists from power.

The mutual interest of India and Central Asia to resolve the Afghan crisis is attested by the results of the First Meeting of the Foreign Ministers at the India-Central Asia Dialogue held in Samarkand in January 2019 with the participation of the Afghan Minister Salahuddin Rabbani. During the meeting of foreign ministers, he reaffirmed the commitment to promoting the economic development of Afghanistan through the implementation of joint infrastructure, transport, energy and other projects that contribute to its inclusion in regional and global economic relations.

At the India-Central Asia Dialogue, following issues were also raised which included enhancing mutual trade; expanding direct contacts between business associations; developing transport and the communication potential of the countries of Central Asia; promoting joint initiatives to create international and regional transport corridors; attracting Indian investments, and promoting innovation and technology in the economies of Central Asia. Following the meeting, a joint ministerial statement of the foreign affairs ministers of the countries participating in the Dialogue was adopted, whereby they confirmed their desire for regional cooperation, mutual support and joint ventures for security, stability and sustainable development. The ministerial meeting once again demonstrated that India and the countries of Central Asia have a common approach to the establishment and development of a multifaceted, mutually beneficial and fruitful cooperation in the format of a Dialogue (MEA, 2019).

Implementation of these plans can also contribute to the Indian transcontinental plan—"North-South Transport Corridor", which is a 7,200 km. multi-modal corridor interconnecting the Indian Ocean, the Persian Gulf and the Caspian Sea. According to the plan, the goods will be transported from Jawaharlal Nehru Port and Port Kandla in western India to Port Bandar Abbas in Iran and further by road and rail through Baku, Moscow and St. Petersburg.

In perspective, a second route may be constructed along the western coast of the Caspian Sea and a new railway link to connect Kazakhstan, Turkmenistan and Iran may also be constructed. Cooperation between Central Asia and India to connect the Kazakhstan-Turkmenistan-Iran and Kazakhstan-Uzbekistan-Turkmenistan-Iran rail routes to the port of Chabahar for the transportation of goods is vital (Jayanth, 2013). This route can drive trade in a region that integrates and develops quickly. In addition, the new route will be 30 percent cheaper and 40 percent shorter than the current sea routes. Hence, one can say, the "North-South Transport Corridor" could become the "Indian version of the Belts and Road initiative" for the countries of Central Asia (Baydarov, 2018).

Cultural and Humanitarian Cooperation

In addition to political and economic cooperation of the Central Asian nations, India attaches great importance to the establishment of cultural and humanitarian cooperation. Currently, India is establishing a wide field for dialogue with stakeholders, in which humanitarian projects aimed at development and interaction, including at the level of public diplomacy, will play an important role. India is mostly using soft power—the motto is the Gandhian principle "the strength of the argument against the argument of strength," in which the principle of practical Indian philosophy-*Ahimsa* (non-violence) is clearly seen. The goal of Indian soft power is to present it as the largest democracy in the world.

The legacy of Buddha, Mahatma Gandhi and the principle of non-violence, yoga, traditional Indian philosophy, medicine, health and nutritional practices and many more are all elements of the cultural matrix of Indian civilization, which have great potential to spread globally and largely need no impetus from the Indian government. With competent management and adaptation to modern times, India can become very influential, since these cultural characteristics greatly enhance the global cultural heritage. Narendra Modi, has overseen a revival in attempts at the spread of Indian influence. He perfectly understands the need for a balance of tradition and innovation.

With its humanitarian projects in Central Asia, India is most of all trying to promote itself in the social sphere. Thus, India's Central Asia Strategy—the Central Asia Connect Policy—provides support for the construction of modern hospitals, universities, IT promotion centres and electronic networks. For example, one such collaboration was the opening in 2014 in the Farkhor district on the border of Tajikistan and Afghanistan, of a military hospital built with the assistance of Indian investment. The cultural and humanitarian synergy of India with Central Asia is based on a solid legal framework. Prospective areas have been identified for further cooperation between countries, such as education, joint research programs, information technology, and tourism.

In Uzbekistan, with the support of India's foreign policy and cultural institutions, new cultural research centres have been opened. Additionally, more than 350 agreements on scientific cooperation with a number of universities and research centres of India have been concluded. Events have been held to promote the dissemination of cultural and scientific information about Indian technological achievements. With Indian financial assistance to the Uzbek University of Information Technology, Muhammad al-Khwarizmi opened the Centre for the use of world achievements in this industry. Thanks to the organization of regular internships for Uzbek citizens in India on courses of the newest technologies and English, every year over 150 interns receive free education in modern specialized centres in New Delhi and other Indian mega-cities.

For Central Asian students, permanent undergraduate, graduate and postgraduate study in various specialties at the largest universities in India is organized through the Indian

Council for Cultural Relations (Indian Council for Cultural Relations, ICCR) [Tashtemkhanova and Orakbayeva, 2017: 49]. The Embassy of India and the Indian Cultural Centre in Uzbekistan and Kazakhstan, have provided financial support in the publication of "A Hindi Textbook for Schools" (in Uzbek) and a Kazakh-Hindi/Hindi-Kazakh dictionary, which is the first textbook in history of Uzbek and Kazakh Indology. Thus, the basis of India's cooperation with the countries of Central Asia is determined by political, economic, cultural and humanitarian factors. It is also necessary to develop other areas of cooperation between India and the countries of Central Asia.

Conclusion

Recent years have shown the development of higher levels of interaction between India and the countries of Central Asia, with the goal being to improve and expand mutual cooperation through the development of more government and private channels of communication. In addition, the foundations of these new relations are not only limited to strategic interests between the countries, but also include taking advantage of new opportunities. In this regard, Connect Central Asia's policy will promote regional cooperation.

One fundamental feature of Indian policy in the region is an emphasis on the development of bilateral interstate cooperation and limited participation in local developments. The changing balance of forces and interests in Central Asia requires a focused approach towards the region. In the medium term, India will continue to attempt to strengthen its strategic position in Central Asia.

References

Bajdarov, E.U. (2018), "India and China Pick up the Key to Central Asia, but in Different Ways", Eurasia.expert, March 21, available at:
http://eurasia.expert/indiya-i-kitay-podbirayut-klyuch-k-tsentralnoy-azii-no-raznymi-sposobami-kazakhstanskiy-ekspert.

Bajdarov, E.U. (2018), "The Competition between the Chinese and Indian Projects in Central Asia is already Underway", Eurasia.expert, April 11, available at: http://eurasia.expert/konkurentsiya-mezhdu-kitayskim-i-indiyskim-proektom-v-tsentralnoy-azii.

Bisaria, Ajay (2013), "Connect Central Asia Policy", in Rashpal Malhotra, Sucha Singh Gill and Neetu Gaur (eds.), 'Perspectives on Bilateral and Regional Cooperation: South and Central Asia', pp. 183-186, Chandigarh: Centre for Rural and Industrial Development (CRRID).

Erekesheva, L.G. (Red.) (2017), "Indija, Kitaj, Central'najaAzija: global'nye, regional'nye, stranovyeaspekty" [India, China, Central Asia: Global, Regional, Country aspects], Almaty, ID MIR, 478.

"Indian Company ONGC is Going to Acquire 40% Stake in Satpayev Oil Field", *Kazakhstan Today*, January 13, 2019, available at: https://www.kt.kz/rus/economy/indijskaja_kompanija_ongc_sobiraetsja_priobresti_40procentnuju_dolju_v_neftjanom_mestorozhdenii_satpaev_1153473872.html.

Jayanth, Jacob (2013), "India, Iran Talk Chabahar Port Funding", *Times of India*, May 5, available at: http://www.hindustantimes.com/world-news/RestOfAsia/I ndia -Iran-talk-Chabahar-port-funding/Article1-1054979.aspx.

Kaushiki, Nishtha (2013), "The New Great Game and India's Connect Central Asia Policy: Strategic Perspectives and Challenges", *Journal of International and Area Studies,* 20(2), pp. 83-100.

"Kazakhstan's Trade with India Reached $1.2 billion", *Kazakhstan News*, February 22, 2019, available at: https://aqparat.info/news/2019/02/22/9168450-tovarooborot_kazahstana_s_indiei_dostig.html.

Orakbaeva, U.M. (2017), "Indian Policy towards Central Asia: Evolution and Dynamics of Changes", thesis for the degree of Doctor of Philosophy (Ph.D.), Astana: L.N. Gumilyov Eurasian National University.

Savkovich, E.V. (2012), "RazvitieotnoshenijIndii s gosudarstvamiCentral'nojAzii v 1990–2000-e gg. ipozicijaKitaja" [The Development of India's Relations with the States of Central Asia in the 1990s-2000s and the Position of China], *VestnikTomskogogosudarstvennogouniversiteta*, Serija

Istorija, 3(19), pp. 114-120.

Stobdan, P. (2005), "Stabilizacija: vid izIndii" [Stabilization: view from India]. *StrategijaRossii* 12, available at: http://sr.fondedin.ru/new/fullnews_arch_to.php?subaction=-showfull-&id=1135069741&archive=1135070770&start_from=&ucat=14&.

Tashtemkhanova, R.M. and Orakbayeva, U.M. (2017), "Cultural Interaction between India and Central Asian States", *VestnikPavlodarskogogosudarstvennogouniversiteta*, Serija, Gumanitarnaja, 2: 46-53.

"The First Ministerial Meeting in Samarkand Ended", Embassy of the Republic of Uzbekistan in the Republic of Kazakhstan, January 13, available at: http://www.uzembassy.kz/ru/article/zavershilas-pervaya-ministerskaya-vstrecha-v-gsamarkande.

Troickij, E.F. (2013), "PolitikaIndii v Central'nojAzii (2001-2012 gg.)", [India's Policy in Central Asia (2001–2012)], *VestnikTomskogogosudarstvennogouniversiteta* 375: 106-108.

6

India-Central Asia Relations and the Stability of Afghanistan Post-2014

Rahul Dev

Introduction

Central Asia is considered to be part of India's extended neighbourhood, and has had strong historical, cultural, and economic relations with India since the time of Silk Route. Unfortunately, the partition of India in 1947 and the disintegration of USSR in 1991 resulted in the drifting away of these five Central Asian Republics (CAR) from India. In this paper, the author will try to analyzc how both India and CAR are important to each other, what role the recently concluded first ever India-Central Asia summit in Uzbekistan can play in that, and how future cooperation can be enhanced.

Despite having huge potential in both regions, their cooperation is below par, having trade of just US$ 2 billion per annum. The constraints between these two regions include air connectivity, security threats, lack of investments, involvement of China through SCO and no direct land connectivity. Both these regions have a huge potential but they must collaborate in the fields of developing hydropower, solar energy, security, tourism, trade, investments, developing joint ventures, and more.

The visit of Indian Prime Minister Mr. Narendra Modi to all five CARs, organizing the first India Central Asia summit in 2019, opening of Chahbar port and India's inclusion in SCO in 2017 in many ways have solved most of the constraints. India already enjoys soft power initiatives in five central Asian republics particularly in the form of Bollywood; however, there are other very significant areas which have been unsuccessful, largely due to Indian government's neglect of the region. In the concluding section, the author would like to throw some light on the issue of Afghanistan—how peace can be developed in Afghanistan with the joint efforts of India and Central Asian countries.

India-Central Asia Historical Relations

India and five Central Asian Republics have enjoyed warm and healthy relationship with each other since times immemorial. Throughout history, Central Asia has formed an important strategic link between the East and the West and has been described as the "great pivot" in the early twentieth century. Central Asia in ancient and medieval times was the crossroad of civilization. The relationship dates back to 3rd Century when India and Central Asia were connected via the Silk Road until the 15th century, when the sea route from Europe to India was discovered. The old "Silk Road" was a major route of connection between these regions and via this route there was exchange of ideas, goods, religion, trade, philosophies and technologies. Central Asia has been at the crossroads of civilizations and trade between the East and the West.

A lot of cities were established along the Silk Road where Indians practiced their culture and religion, having their own social and political organizations, and having distinct language, scripts, literature, philosophy, art and architecture (Kothari, 2014). India has always been a lucrative land for scholars, saints, philosophers, traders and invaders. It is a well-known fact that Sufism came to India from Central Asia and that cities like Bukhara and Samarkand were centres of Sufi saints. Some Central Asian scholars who visited India during this period include Al-Beruni, Zia-ul Din Nakhsbandi, Abdurrazzak Samarqandi and Al-Kharezmi. There is evidence that Central Asia had contact with the ancient Indian Indus valley civilization. Various archaeological excavations have found items like pottery, ivory and metal goods belonging to the Harappan culture that shows India's contact with ancient Central Asia.

Medieval Central Asia was a land of foreign invasion on India. The first Mughal emperor Babur came from the Ferghana Valley after losing his kingdom to try his fortune in India and also medieval India was ruled by others from Central Asia, like Genghis Khan, Timur, and Mohammad Gori who plundered and looted India (Gopal, 2001: 72-75). India and Central Asia shared the common bond of Buddhism. The arrival of Buddhism in Central Asia opened a new chapter of contact between the two regions. Buddhism was born in India but from Central Asia, Buddhism expanded to China, Korea and Japan. The Silk Road played a pivotal role in the spread of Buddhism in Central Asia and China before the advent of Islam.

Regarding the spread of Buddhism in Central Asia, Dr. M. Kh. Abuseitova explains, "The spread of Buddhism in Central Asia under the Kushans was accompanied not by blind acceptance of the ideas of ancient Indian culture, but by their understanding and combination with local cultural traditions". The Kushan Empire and the acceptance of Buddhism by King Ashok himself gave impetus to the spread of Buddhism in Central Asia. Before the advent of Islam, Central Asia was the cradle of Buddhist civilization. Later on, Central Asia became a hub of Islamic civilization. Many Indian freedom fighters like Bankim Chandra Chatterji, Bhagat Singh and Tagore were inspired by the events of the 1917 October Revolution in their struggle against the British. Liberty, equality and fraternity became the basis of new ways of life for both the people of Central Asia and India, post-1947 Indian independence (Ahmar, 1992: 57-70).

India-Central Asia Relations Post-Cold War

The partition of India in 1947 pushed Central Asia away from India and having no direct land connectivity, became the main stumbling block in further developing relations between them. During the Cold War, India and Central Asia enjoyed a warm relationship. Political contacts grew and expanded with a frequent exchange of visits by the top leaders. Visit by the first Prime Minister of India Pandit Jawaharlal Nehru to Almaty Tashkent and Ashgabat in 1955 brought the two regions closer to each other. Later on, in 1960, the first secretary of Soviet Union, Nikita Khruschev visited India and thereafter there were frequent exchange of visits between both heads of the state which continues in present times as well.

The current Indian Prime Minister Narendra Modi is the only one who in his five years tenure has visited all the five Central Asian republics in a single visit. During the Soviet period, culture, music, dance, movies and literature bound the Soviet republics closely with India. But the relationship suffered a huge setback and neglect for the last 25 years following the disintegration of the Soviet Union in 1991. The end of the Cold War changed the geopolitical map of the world with the emergence of fifteen new republics. Russia as the successor state of USSR, inherited its military might, nuclear power, and its membership to the United Nations Security Council (Singh, 1995: 69-72).

Indian foreign policy makers saw Russia after the Cold War as a great land of opportunities and tried to promote their relations with Russia thereby neglecting the Central Asian Republics as India was unsure of their stability and survival. India found Russia much closer to it, which led to the signing of Indo-Soviet Friendship Treaty in 1971, thereby formalizing the Soviet stance on many issues like independence of Bangladesh, India's claim over Kashmir, defence deals, the common threat of the *Taliban* emanating from Afghanistan and the United States nexus with Pakistan to fund the *Taliban* through Central Intelligence agency (CIA) against the Soviets in Afghanistan. However, the changing regional scenario over the last decade has prompted India to change its stance over Central Asia which they had ignored for almost 25 years.

India is trying to develop its relations with Central Asia

through its "Connect Central Asia Policy" which was announced by India's Minister of State for External Affairs Mr. E. Ahamed on June 12, 2012 in Bishkek (Kyrgyzstan) in his first keynote address at the first India-Central Asia Dialogue. India considers Central Asia as being its extended neighbourhood and wants to develop cooperation in hydropower, solar energy, security cooperation, tourism, trade, investments, science and technology and utility of its abundant energy resources to fulfil its growing energy needs. It is in India's best interest to promote economic and security cooperation with Central Asia to act as a bulwark against Pakistan and China in the future. Post-9/11, the importance of Central Asia has grown dramatically.

The involvement of foreign players in the region has made it an arena of the "New Great Game of 21st Century" where all regional and extra regional powers are competing for their personal interests. The US needs Central Asian help in its war on terror in Afghanistan and China wants to expand its clout over the region to obtain Asian hegemony and achieve its dream of reviving a new Silk Road and its Belt and Road initiatives (BRI) by using a policy of debt trap. Russia is actively seeking to rebuild its economic influence via the newly created Eurasian Economic Union and to counter the US presence in Central Asia. Pakistan wants more influence in Central Asia where it can support and harbour anti-Indian activities from Central Asia and support terrorist organizations to wage war against India for the liberation of Kashmir.

India is a latecomer in the region. India in its quest for regional and economic security has started to focus its attention on Central Asia, due to abundant hydrocarbon reserves and the Chinese strategy of encirclement of India. These tensions have added further strains on India's ambitions to enhance its strategic profile in Central Asia. 2019 will be a watershed year for India-Central Asia relations. The first India-Central Asia summit was held on January 11 and 12, 2019 in Samarkand, Uzbekistan, where all five heads of the

Central Asian countries, and India's External Affairs Minister Sushma Swaraj were present, and the proposed SCO summit was held on June 13 and 14, 2019 in Kyrgyzstan. This new shift marks a change in India's approach to Central Asia which has been inadequate so far.

India's Aims and Interests in Central Asia

India has three main objectives in Central Asia: increased security, greater political influence and enhanced economic development. A stable Central Asia is necessary for India to further enhance its bilateral relationship. The countries of Central Asia are endowed with significant hydrocarbon and mineral resources which are important for India to fulfil its growing energy needs. In order to meet the expectations, India launched the Connect Central Asia Policy in 2012. According to India's former Minister of State for External Affairs, the Connect Central Asia Policy has three main themes: political, economic and people to people engagement with Central Asian countries, both individually, and collectively. With the entry of India, a "New Great Game" is developing in Central Asia involving Russia, China, America, Pakistan and Iran. America sees India as a balancing factor against Russia and China (Usha, 2012). Central Asia's vast oil and gas resources and its strategic location as a bridge between Asia and the Middle East have invited severe competition among far-flung and regional players.

India's main concern in Central Asia is security; any instability in Afghanistan will have spill over effects on Central Asia which will thwart India's interests there. All the Central Asian states are landlocked and India has no direct land connectivity. Central Asia is in need of good relationship with its neighbours and other powers of the world. India's main concern in Central Asia is that it shares border with both Pakistan and Afghanistan. Pakistan is a hostile neighbour and always supports anti-Indian activities. Pakistan wants an unstable Afghanistan ruled by the *Taliban* so that it can continue its policy of terror against India.

India knows that an Afghanistan ruled by the *Taliban* will support terrorism in Jammu and Kashmir. Post-US withdrawal in 2014, terrorism has increased in Afghanistan; the *Taliban,* supported by Pakistan, is eagerly waiting to come to power in Afghanistan. Afghanistan always blames Pakistan for terrorism in Afghanistan, including attacks on the Afghan parliament and Afghan security forces, which Pakistan denies. Another Indian concern is the penetration of ISIS in Central Asia. It has been estimated that around 10,000 youth from these countries have joined ISIS. India knows that Central Asia can become a breeding ground for ISIS due to its close cultural, religious and geographical proximity with Pakistan. Illegal arms, drugs and human trafficking are also a matter of security concern for India. India believes that money generated from them is being used by terrorists to carry on anti-Indian activities and fuel insurgency in Kashmir.

The other main objective of India in Central Asia is economic. India is late to the arena whereas China and Russia have already made inroads in Central Asia. Huge hydrocarbon reserves and its geostrategic location make Central Asia a land of opportunities. Energy hungry India knows that only Central Asia can fulfil its growing energy needs (Azhar, 2016: 116-129). Kazakhstan has the world's second largest reserves of uranium, and has substantial reserves of minerals including coal, gas, iron ore, zinc, gold and more. Turkmenistan is endowed with the world's fourth largest reserves of natural gas. Kyrgyzstan and Tajikistan have huge hydroelectric potential. Uzbekistan has large reserves of gas, uranium and gold. Since 1991, both India and Central Asian countries have collaborated in various sectors like pharmaceuticals, textiles, metallurgy, chemicals, hydrocarbons, mining, mineral processing, construction and industrial production. However, their trade has been insufficient, just US$ 2 billion per annum. (Rakhimov, 2013: 27-28).

Currently, India wants more collaboration and joint

ventures in fields such as hydropower, solar energy, security cooperation, tourism, trade investments, banking, space exploration, nuclear deals, IT sector and increasing people to people contact etc. Over the last few years, especially since 2014, India has stepped up its engagement with the Central Asian Republics, with the aim of building long-term partnerships in the region. High-level visits from both sides over the last few years are testimony to the fact that there is growing political, economic and defence ties between India and Central Asia. The first such step in this direction was the culmination of the India-Central Asia dialogue, a Track-II initiative organized on June 12-13, 2012, in Bishkek, Kyrgyzstan, towards building a long-term partnership with the region. The first landmark development in the process of building strategic partnership started when Indian Prime Minister visited all the five Central Asian countries from July 6 to 13, 2015. Some of the agreements signed between Indian Prime Minister and Central Asian states are as follows:

- Kazakhstan President Nursultan Nazarbayev's decision to sign a major contract for a renewed long-term supply of 5,000 metric tons (MT) of uranium to India over the next five years is the most significant takeaway of the Prime Minister's visit.
- India's ONGC Videsh Ltd. (OVL) had its first breakthrough when Modi launched the drilling operations for oil exploration in the Satpayev region on July 7, 2015.
- Central Asian countries agreed with India in building a North-South transport corridor which will help India bypass Pakistan and reach Central Asia.
- There were deals in strengthening the defence sector and Tajikistan accepted India's demand to upgrade Ayni air base in Tajikistan.
- A memorandum of understanding on cooperation in the field of tourism was signed between the Ministry of Tourism of India and the Ministry of Culture, Information and Tourism of the Government of Kyrgyz Republic.

- There were agreements on skill development, human resource opening in Indian banks, increasing air connectivity, cooperation in fields of culture, information technology, food industry and combating the menace of extremism and terrorism (Stobdan, 2015).

In a bid to improve India-Central Asia relations further, India proposed the first ever India-Central Asia dialogue which was concluded in January 2019 in Samarkand, Uzbekistan. The dialogue was co-chaired by External Affairs Minister Sushma Swaraj and the foreign minister of Uzbekistan, Abdulaaziz Kamilov. The Foreign Ministers of Kyrgyzstan, Tajikistan, Turkmenistan and Kazakhstan participated in the event. The most highlighted feature of this dialogue was the presence of the Afghan External Affairs Minister as a special invitee. India considers Afghanistan to be a vital link in establishing its relationship with Central Asia. India reiterated its commitment to establish peace and security in Afghanistan and promote an Afghan-led, Afghan-owned and Afghan-controlled peace and reconciliation process. As India does not hold talks with *Taliban* officially, it indicated its support for an inclusive peace process in Afghanistan. Some of the key highlights of this dialogue were the following:

- Developing viable connectivity options between India and Central Asia and Afghanistan and Central Asia to further boost trade.
- Strengthen India's engagement, including political, economic, and cultural, with all Central Asian countries and to take it to a new level.
- There was discussion in areas of cooperation like industry, energy, information technology, pharmaceuticals, agriculture, and education.
- Both India and Central Asia pledged to assist Afghanistan in reconstruction and building of infrastructure and other energy projects.
- They also reiterated their support in developing Chabahar port in Iran to facilitate trade among India, Afghanistan

and Central Asia and building of rail linkages in Afghanistan to connect it to Central Asia.

The other area where India wants to foster close relationships are political and cultural. India already employs soft power in Central Asia, and had since the Soviet era when Indian movies, cuisine, dance, literature and music were quite popular in Central Asia. The popularity of iconic Bollywood stars like Raj Kapoor, Nargis, Mithun Chakraborty among others have brought India into the homes and hearts of the common people of this region. India also employs its soft power in Central Asia in the form of giving loans, humanitarian aid, infrastructure development, joint military exercises, and medical assistance to the Central Asian states and Afghanistan. India uses soft power in shaping the values, beliefs and attitudes of a cross-section of the world population. India uses all its cultural, spiritual and political heritage in building links with Central Asia, as for example, *yoga, ayurveda* (the traditional system of Hindu medicine), Buddhist, Sufi and Hindu ideas and the philosophies and ideologies of non-violent protest and non-cooperation have been showcased to bolster India's image in Central Asia.

Despite all this, India's position in Central Asia is quite weak compared to China and Russia. China also employs soft power by way of economic aid, cultural exchange and providing scholarships to students of Central Asian countries and building hospitals and mosques in Afghanistan. In comparison to Indian soft power, the Chinese soft power is much more visible and effective as it is backed by hard power. Professor Joseph Nye (2004) argues that soft power must be backed by hard power to realize its goals; without using hard power, soft power is of no use, and there should be a carrot and stick policy. India must use a combination of both hard and soft power to realize its goals in the region and to counter the Chinese and Pakistani influence.

To cement its political ties with Central Asia, India started its Connect Central Asia Policy in June 2012. In the political sphere, India has to face manifold challenges which include stabilizing Afghanistan, countering China, the fight against Islamic fundamentalism, cooperation with US in its war on terror, and keeping out Pakistan and collaborating with the Shanghai Cooperation Organization (SCO). It has been estimated that the withdrawal of US forces from the region will further escalate terrorist threats emanating from Afghanistan which is a huge matter of concern for India, China and Russia. In Kashmir, Xinjiang, and Chechnya, India, China and Russia are fighting against a common enemy. The main constraint here is Pakistan which blocks India geographically and politically. China through its close relationship with Pakistan and its US$ 44 billion investment in Gwadar port in Baluchistan, is attempting to isolate India internationally.

The opening of Chabahar Port in collaboration with Iran as a counter to the Sino-Pakistani nexus has in many ways reduced India's dependence on Pakistan to reach out to Central Asia via Afghanistan. The proposed TAPI pipeline has been suspended due to hostile relations between India and Pakistan. However, all the paper work and formalities have been completed. The TAPI pipeline is an idea that existed since 1997 but had not been started due to instability in Afghanistan and Pakistan's reluctance to ratify it (Blank, 2014).

Now, this would force India to turn to Iran for energy supply which will displease the US, as America is continuously pressing India to stop all commercial and trade links with Iran. America's tension with Iran is well known due to its nuclear plans and its hostility towards Saudi Arabia. Another constraint here for India is the Chinese backed SCO. China by playing the SCO card is attempting to bring the Central Asian states under its wing.

However, in 2017, it granted permanent membership to both India and Pakistan. India needs to solve the above-mentioned challenges to really reap the benefit of its Connect Central Asia Policy which looks dismal post-US withdrawal, amid developing Chinese, Russian and Pakistani roles in the region. The current Indian government, headed by Prime Minister Modi, has a foreign policy that has been inclined to establish relations with US, Israel and France. The Indian government's neglect of its traditional partners like Russia has prompted Russia, China and Pakistan to create a new alliance. Russia has recently sold arms to Pakistan, and conducted their first ever joint military exercise named *Druzba*in 2016 despite India's objections, after the attack on the Pathankot air base in Jammu and Kashmir, of which India has accused Pakistan's involvement.

India, Central Asian States and Stability in Afghanistan

Due to Afghanistan's geostrategic location, the multiethnic and multilingual country has long been an area of competition for imperial powers since the 19th century. Competition and rivalry among the imperial powers to gain control over Afghanistan has devastated it in many ways. Stability in Afghanistan is of paramount importance for both India and Central Asia. Afghan stability today depends more than ever on relations between regional states rather than on the role of world powers. So far, Afghanistan has succeeded in maintaining a balanced relationship with both global and regional powers (Patnaik, 2016: 29-34).

The proximity of Afghanistan with Central Asia, and its geostrategic location makes it an important entity for Indian policy makers. Following the overthrow of the Taliban regime at the end of 2001 by US-led coalition, India has provided substantial assistance to Afghanistan for economic development, training, and capacity building amounting to more than US$ 2.3 billion. Broadly speaking, New Delhi has pursued a "soft power" strategy towards Afghanistan, sticking to civilian rather than military matters. In consonance with the priorities laid down by the Hamid Karzai government, Indian assistance has focused on building human capital and physical infrastructure, improving security, and helping the agricultural and other important sectors of the country's economy. The

Indian government is building roads, mosques, hospitals, dams, providing medical facilities, and helping with educational programs, in an effort to develop and enhance long-term Afghan capabilities. India has been involved in the following projects in Afghanistan (Astri, 2007: 1291-1308).

- India constructed the 218 km. Zaranj-Delaram road in remote south-western Afghanistan with the help of Border Roads Organization (BRO) at a cost of US$ 84 million in 2009 and the road is linked with Iran which helps Afghanistan facilitate trade with the Gulf countries.
- India has established various medical missions in Kabul, Mazar-e-Sharif, Herat, Jalalabad, and Kandahar, with around 15 doctors treating more than 3.5 lakh patients every year since 2003, and has reconstructed the Indira Gandhi Institute for Child Health in Kabul.
- India is reconstructing the Salma Dam Power Project in Herat province at an estimated cost of US$ 109.3 million which will provide 42 MW of power to the Herat province. The project involves the erection of 110 KV power transmission lines from Salma Dam to Herat city over a distance of 143 kms.
- India is supplying 100 grams of fortified, high protein biscuits to nearly 2 million children daily, under a school feeding program, and provided 250,000 metric tonnes of wheat in 2009 to help Afghanistan to cope up with its food crisis.
- India constructed the new Afghan parliament building in 2009.
- Some Indian activities in the education and capacity development sector include: reconstruction and renovation of Habiba School in Kabul, award of 500 Indian Council for Cultural Relations (ICCR) long-term university scholarships for graduate and post-graduate programs in India annually.
- India's other short-term projects include training Afghan police officers, diplomats and civil servants. They are also

providing technical support in the areas of transportation, power, telecommunication and irrigation projects and providing technical assistance to women's vocational training centre at Bagh-e-Zanana in Kabul (Pant, 2010: 133-153).

India has very clearly stated that any reconciliation process in Afghanistan should be Afghan-led as it fears Pakistan interjection in the process would see the rise of groups considered to be its strategic assets. India is worried that the security vacuum left behind by the US military is being filled by the Taliban and supported by Pakistan and there has been a surge in militancy in Jammu and Kashmir, as was the case when the Taliban was in power from 1996-2001. The opportunities that Afghanistan presents to India are unique in many ways. Afghanistan is important to India for its energy security as it is the gateway to energy rich Central Asia. India is involved in three iron ore projects in Hajigak in Afghanistan and their security is quite challenging, as many Indian workers and diplomats have been killed in Afghanistan (Katju, 2013). A stable and friendly Afghanistan will enable India to fight the menace of narco-terrorism and illegal arms trade that threatens India's internal security.

A stronger Indian presence in Afghanistan will help it check Pakistani influence in Afghanistan by engaging Pakistan on its western border. India is also cooperating with Russia and Iran to achieve its objectives and is trying to build the New Delhi-Moscow-Tehran axis to address the Afghan problem. As a friendly gesture to bring Afghanistan into South Asian mainstream, India granted South Asian Association Cooperation (SAARC) membership to Afghanistan in 2007 to facilitate the free flow of goods, thereby leading to greater economic development in the region (Roy, 2010: 545-561). Being a landlocked state, Afghanistan security and stability depends upon its neighbours and vice-versa. The Central Asian Republics breathed a sigh of relief after the ouster of the Taliban from Afghanistan in 2001.

Since 2001, the Central Asian Republics have contributed immensely to the stability of Afghanistan by providing military bases, opening transit routes to coalition forces and providing humanitarian assistance to Afghanistan. A Taliban controlled Afghanistan has long threatened the security of the CARs. The Taliban supported the Islamic Movement of Uzbekistan (IMU) by providing them training, funding, weapons, and hiding places. The Islamic Movement of Uzbekistan and the Taliban actively worked to destabilize Central Asia in order to establish Islamic *Shariat* rule like in Afghanistan. The Central Asian States resisted the Taliban and were the first to support the US-led coalition forces. Uzbekistan was the first country to provide military bases to the US air force to carry out operations in Afghanistan as early as September 22, 2001.

Soon, Kyrgyzstan followed suit and provided Manas airport to carry out offensive and humanitarian operations. Kazakhstan also offered Almaty airport for US military aircraft after having heated consultations with Russia. Turkmenistan, which follows a policy of neutrality and Tajikistan, also offered their support to US led forces for humanitarian and military operations. The CAR's and India post-US withdrawal from Afghanistan in 2014 have supported Afghanistan in all possible ways including humanitarian aid, training Afghan security personnel, doctors, civil servants and technicians, combating weapons and arms trafficking by reopening their consulates in Afghanistan, and by supporting the new regime in Afghanistan headed by Ashraf Ghani (Maan, 2003: 62-69).

Conclusion

Afghanistan borders three Central Asian countries and a volatile situation in Afghanistan may have spill over effects on India as well as the whole of Central Asia. Both India and Central Asia must collaborate in bringing peace to Afghanistan and attempting to combat common threats emanating from

Afghanistan in the form of terrorism, drug trafficking, arms trafficking, and the penetration of ISIS. To conclude, the Central Asian Republics and India have played a very important role by rendering their support to US-led war on terrorism and rebuilding 30 years war torn Afghanistan.

The Taliban/Al-Qaida, IMU and ISIS network has been destroyed. The Afghanistan is on the path of development, democratization and rebuilding, the prospects of stable government are achievable with the long-term continuous cooperation of Afghanistan with CAR and India. Under the Bonn Agreement, all the Central Asian Republics have pledged their support to building a new Afghanistan, led and owned by Afghans. The onus is now on regional powers like India, China and the Central Asian Republics to bring stability and peace in Afghanistan. A stable and democratic Afghanistan in future will ensure the stability and security of CAR and India.

References

Ahmar, Moonis (1992), "India and its Role in New Central Asia", *Pakistan Horizon.*

Azhar, Muhammad (2016), "Trade between India and Central Asia", in Nasir Raza Khan (ed.), 'India, Central Asia and the World Powers', Delhi: Primus Books.

Gopal, Surendra (2001), "India and Central Asia: Cultural, Economic and Political Links", Delhi: Shipra Publications.

Katju, Vivek (2013), "The Many Roads to Kabul", *The Hindu,* New Delhi, October 15.

Kothari, Raj Kumar (2014), "India's 'Connect Central Asia Policy': Emerging Economic and Security Dimensions", *Sociology and Anthropology*, Vol. 2(6), pp. 239-245.

Maan, Poonam (2003), "The Role of Neighbours: Central Asian Republics", in Sreedhar (ed.), 'Afghanistan in Transistion', New Delhi: Indian Council of World Affairs.

Nye, Jr. Joseph (2004), "Soft Power: The Means to Success in World Politics", New York: Public.

Pant. V. Harsh (2010), "India in Afghanistan: A Test Case for Rising Power", *Contemporary South Asia,* Vol. 18, No, 2, June, pp.

133-153.

Patnik, Ajay (2016), "Central Asia: Geopolitics, Security and Stability", New York: Routledge.

Rakhimov, Mirzokhid (2013), "Regional Cooperation in Central Asia and Perspective of Central Asia-India Relations", in Nasir Raza Khan (ed.), 'India, Central Asia and the World Powers', Delhi: Primus Books.

Roy, Singh Meena (2010), "The Role of SCO in Afghanistan: Scope and Limitations", *Strategic Analysis,* 34(4), pp. 545-561.

Singh, Anita, Inder (1995), "India's Relation with Russia and Central Asia", *International Affairs*, Vol. 71, No. 1, pp. 69-81.

Stobdan, P. (2015), "Central Asia: India's Northern Exposure", IDSA Monograph Series, No. 44. New Delhi: Institute for Defence Studies and Analyses.

Suhrke, Astri (2007), "Reconstruction as Modernization: The Post-conflict Project in Afghanistan", *Third World Quarterly,* Vol. 25, (7), pp. 1291- 1308.

Usha, K.B. (2012), "India's Foreign Policy Priorities in Central Asia", *Foreign Policy Research Centre (FPRC) Journal*, 10(2), p. 104.

7

Building Relations between India and Central Asia

Zhansaya Zhangabulova

Introduction

Central Asia has long been a zone of Indian influence. India currently has close contacts with five states in the region. Over the centuries, powerful regimes similar to those of Central Asia have repeatedly appeared and disappeared there. That is, they are ethnically Turkic, culturally Iranian-Tajik, and Muslim. They have left an indelible mark on India. History is full of positive interactions between Indians and the inhabitants of Central Asia due to the movement of people, goods and ideas, and a strong spiritual influence.

Relations between India and Central Asia, especially Kazakhstan, have recently become more active. The population of Central Asia has tremendous sympathy for Indian culture. In other words, Central Asian society is open to the Indian experience. It would be unreasonable to ignore this factor, when considering the introduction and favourable conditions for the formation of an open society, and democratic values in the region. Since the establishment of diplomatic relations, India and Central Asia have signed a number of framework agreements on cooperation in the fields of culture, commerce, economics, civil aviation, investment promotion, and security. Foreign ministry consultations often help facilitate fruitful discussions on bilateral and international issues.

Today, India's Central Asia policy is largely formed; institutionalization and some transformation is now the priority due to external and internal factors. The renewal of India's policies in the area is determined by its proximity to Afghanistan and the presence of possible security threats, such as the proliferation of narco-trafficking, terrorism and religious extremism, which have spread in the region. The Indian establishment is also pushing for the pursuit of a more intensive Central Asia policy due to fear related to the steady rise of Chinese financial and military power. In addition to bilateral opportunities for cooperation, India has some useful tools to increase its influence in the region. In this regard, India's regional policy priorities, as well as key tools and mechanisms for their implementation in general, are of particular importance.

At present, the interests of a number of states meet in Central Asia. The region has been isolated for a long time, being an integral part of the Russian Empire. However, in the future, both its geopolitical role and the intensity of the struggle of external forces for dominance seem to grow. Many states consider Central Asia as a vital zone of national interests. The United States, the EU, Russia, China, India, and Arab countries have shown interest in the region, although the degree of this interest and the possibilities to provide it vary widely.

Everything that happens in the region has always directly affected the national security of neighbouring geopolitical centres of power. Significant reserves of strategically important resources, mainly sources of energy such as fossil fuels, which are of strategic interest to both Russia and the West, and to the growing economies of China and India are concentrated in Central Asia. At the same time, the Central Asian region has historically been a transport and communications hub along the East-West and North-South routes, the volume of trade along these routes is vital to all the nations mentioned above.

Along with the gradual transition from a bipolar world order to a multi-polar one and also after the collapse of the

USSR, the development of national institutions in Central Asia continues, and, accordingly, their transformation as participants in global international relations. We are observing the formation of statehood in a modern sense of the word, which is inherent in democratic, civilized societies, socially oriented market economies and independent foreign policies pursued in accordance with generally accepted principles of international law. But these states are still at the very beginning of this path, and therefore their foreign policies are characterized in many aspects by inconsistency, instability and in a certain sense, unpredictability. However, the strength of their foreign policies is greatly influenced by external factors, namely intervention by Russia, the USA and China.

Central Asia on the World Map

Central Asia has been witnessing an increased role in world economy and politics, as shown by an increasing interest by a number of states in it, including India. This had long been an area of over-land trade stretching from China and India to the Middle East. In Soviet times, the concept of "Central Asia" referred to the region around Mongolia, and the concept of "Middle Asia" was separated from it (the latter did not include Kazakhstan).

The concept of Central Asia emerged after the collapse of the USSR in the terminology of modern international relations. However, there are alternative definitions, for example, "Greater Central Asia", which includes Afghanistan, the north-western part of India, and even part of Pakistan. There are many other cultural, historical, geo-economic and geopolitical names of the region. Their struggle is a symbolic and ideological dimension of the "New Big Game", the participants of which are the great powers fighting for regional influence.

The first President of Kazakhstan, Nursultan Nazarbayev, proposed abandoning the definition of "Middle Asia and Kazakhstan" in favour of the concept of "Central Asia" covering all the post-Soviet states of this region at the summit of the states of Central Asia in 1992 (Shabalin, 2018).

Kazakhstan historically was not a part of Central (by Western definition) or Middle (by Russian-Soviet definition) Asia. In the traditional geographical and political sense, it is a part of Inner Asia, that is, the region that separates East Asia from Central and Eastern Asia (Anterior and Middle Asia or Near and Middle East). Central Asia (in the modern sense) and Middle Asia (in the Russian-Soviet sense), is one and the same. The only difference is that the first one now includes Kazakhstan, and the second one does not.

In a word, currently Central Asia as a geographical-political concept is an invention of the post-Soviet period. In Soviet times, Kazakhstan wasn't a part of Central Asia. After the collapse of Soviet Socialist power, Middle Asia in an international context was transformed into Central Asia. And Kazakhstan was fastened to it on the grounds that it was necessary to designate one name to the Trans-Caspian region. Transcaucasia is now South Caucasus, and Kazakhstan and Middle Asia are now designated Central Asia (Maksudov, 2018).

American sources have mentioned Central Asia since the 19th century. One of the prominent American sources about Central Asia is the research work "Turkestan", written by American Geographer and diplomat Eugene Schuyler (1840-1890) (Kazantsev, 2003). As the American Consul in Moscow and Secretary of the American Embassy in St. Petersburg in 1867-1875, he visited many regions of Russia, was a member of the Russian Geographical Society, and actively studied the political and cultural aspects of the Russian society. By the time he visited Turkestan, which had long been an integral part of the Russian Empire; his research was of no small importance to the development of historical, geographical and political studies in the United States, which was undergoing a period of reconstruction and abolition of slavery.

Schuyler observed changes in Russian society after the

abolition of serfdom in 1861. He made a comparative analysis of the socio-political development that took place in two diametrically opposed societies (Kydyrbekuly, 2003). Until the European discovery of the New World, Central Asia had been the key axis of the Eurasian continent, connecting the countries of the Far East through Europe, the Middle and Near East, and South Asia by the Great Silk Road. Control over land transport communications and the mobility of Central Asian nomads made it possible to create great empires in antiquity and the Middle Ages, and largely determined the course of Eurasian history.

Mutual Penetration and Clash of Interests in Central Asia

After the collapse of the Soviet Union, the region, previously closed to external influence, once again became an arena for conflicts of interest between the great powers. The international community is attracted to the rich raw materials of Central Asia, and its key position in the heart of the Eurasian continent, makes it possible to realize new transcontinental transport corridors that help form a new regional geopolitical reality.

However, today, Central Asian countries need effective financing for small and medium-sized businesses, which currently have the potential to carry out institutional and policy reforms, as well as create new jobs. Also, it is worth mentioning that countries in the region have reduced the costs of education after gaining independence and has had a significant impact on the quality of education. The system of attitudes does not meet the employer's requirements, and the professional knowledge is poorly financed. Human capital in these countries is less developed than ever.

All of this is due to the fact that the development of production and economic competitiveness of Central Asian countries is aggravating. Nonetheless, Central Asia is adjacent to most of the Caspian Sea basin. Its proven fuel resources (not including the share of Iran) are currently estimated at 85 billion barrels (11.6 billion tenge) of oil, with a potential of about 100 billion barrels (13.6 billion tenge). American experts cite lower rates of proven reserves of Caspian oil (2.5-5 billion tenge), but they estimate potentially higher reserves.

The total potential of the energy resources of Central Asia is as follows: more than 12 trillion tons of natural gas m^3 (about 5 trillion m^3 explored), gas condensate about 1 billion tons, and oil about 13 billion tons. There are explored coal reserves exceeding 4 billion tons (Prokofiev, 2005). According to the US National Security Strategy of 1997, "The stable and prosperous states of the Caucasus and Central Asia will help establish stability and security from the Mediterranean to China, promote rapid development, and transport large Caspian oil and gas with a substantial commercial participation of the United States" (A National Security Strategy for a New Washington, D.C.: The White House, 1997).

Central Asia: A Zone of Indian Influence

Republic of India is one of the few countries in the world, which both locally and internationally surpasses in geography and population spheres. History of India is also varied and rich. In modern India, archaeological evidence has proven that humanity survived since the Stone Age. It is a wonderful country whose part of territory was ruled and prospered by the Mughul Empire. The name "Moghuls" appeared under the British colonialists, neither the founder of the Empire, nor his descendants had not called themselves like that (Zahir-ud-din Mohammad Babur, The Baburnama: Memoirs of Babur, Prince and Emperor, 2002).

The term "Moghul" was used by the people in India to refer to all the Muslims of Northern India and Central Asia (N.K. Sinha and A.C. Banerjee, History of India, 1954). Akbar the Great established himself as a patron of science, art and architecture. Based on the principle of toleration, he gathered around his throne best scholars, poets, musicians and artists who adhered to different religions. During the reign of Akbar, a painting school was created, and the walls of its palaces were decorated with frescoes. Thanks to him, the richest library was assembled. Nevertheless, he was a legendary ruler who sang songs of love and dance and was a symbol of love.

India had a lot in common with Central Asia. Over the centuries, powerful regimes similar to those in Central Asia rose and fell. That is, they were ethnically Turkic, culturally Iranian-Tajik, and Muslims who left a mark on India. There is a long history of friendly interaction between Indians and the inhabitants of Central Asia due to the movement of people and goods and also the spiritual influence.

Mahatma Gandhi, a genius, opined, "we need to change in order to change the world". Obviously, Kazakhstan and India have much in common in their historical mission, and their desire to break through in the civilizational world and share their interests. It was also important and meaningful that the state visit of the first President of the Republic of Kazakhstan, Nursultan Nazarbayev, coincided with the national holiday of the Republic of India, the Independence Day.

Kazakhstan and India have long had a productive relationship. The economic and geographical position of India is characterized by its favourable economic development. Maritime routes range from the Mediterranean Sea to the South Pacific, linking the country to the Pacific Ocean, and connecting it with the states of Indian Ocean and Australia. The Silk Road, which ran through Kazakhstan, ends in India. Ideas about peace and development, largely transmitted by Buddhism in earlier times, are still relevant. For centuries, the Indian people, as well as the people of Kazakhstan, have always accepted people of different faiths in their land. Such communication has yielded positive results in the sense of enrichment through ideas, knowledge and worldview. This combination of culture and different religions has given our people inner strength and unique national character.

India and Kazakhstan established diplomatic relations during the visit of the first President of Kazakhstan Nursultan

Nazarbayev in February 1992. It is not by chance that India was the first country Nazarbayev visited. Despite its small population, Kazakhstan, like India, is a multi-lingual, multi-cultural state with many languages, religions, cultures and nationalities. This has long determined the common interests of the two countries in their domestic and foreign policy and can be of mutual benefit. The dynamics of the development of relations between these countries since 1992 has met these expectations.

Researchers postulate that the historical component of relations between India and Central Asia has laid the foundation for cooperation and forms the basis for further development of relations. In recent years, India has retained a stable seventh place in GDP growth of more than 7 percent and is a leading country in the development of information technology, not to mention its huge human resources (Analytical Portal Humanitarian Technologies, 2018). As its foreign policy resources grow, India's influence will expand into neighbouring regions, including Central Asia. At present, the significance of Central Asia to India lies not only in the civilizational, cultural and historical aspect, rather there is also an increasing attention being paid to geopolitical and economic areas of cooperation.

India's foreign policy today sees its environment as an extension of the circles of interaction and in this context, Central Asia is referred to as an "extended neighbourhood" (Mukherjee, 2006). Recent years have seen more inclusive levels of interaction between India and Central Asia with a desire to improve and expand mutual cooperation through governmental and non-governmental meetings, as well as through contacts between individuals. In addition, the foundations of these new relations are not limited to strategic interests between the two countries, but also regards the new business opportunities. In this regard, Indian policy to connect with Central Asia will promote regional cooperation.

In order to establish strong relations between India and

Central Asia, it is advisable to comprehend the dynamics of bilateral relations. India has close, warm relations with all the Central Asian states. Initially, Uzbekistan was considered a key partner of India in Central Asia. However, greater stability, economically and politically, has played a key role in India shifting its focus from Uzbekistan towards Kazakhstan and Kyrgyzstan. Today, Kazakhstan and Kyrgyzstan have become important partners and play a prominent role in strengthening New Delhi's position in the region.

Foreign Policy of India and Central Asian Republics

Central Asia has become the main focus of India's attention in regional and global interests. Therefore, it can be stated that the current policy of India towards CARs is at the stage of active institutionalization. Economic cooperation is a key factor in Indo-Central Asian relations. Currently, Central Asian countries are open and diversifying their economies. India shares its expertise in areas such as software, services, IT and education. Investments, technological developments and the improvement of the quality of human resources in the region are mutually beneficial. However, despite numerous agreements and memorandums of understanding, India is not one of the leading countries involved in the development of oil and gas resources in Central Asia. So far, the basis of India's cooperation with Central Asia is motivated by political and economic factors. Nevertheless, it is necessary to develop other areas of cooperation between the two regions. It is necessary to further develop cultural and humanitarian cooperation. India's advantage is that it can use soft power and its favourable regional image to strengthen bilateral ties in different areas.

India apparently considers there to be a mutual ground, primarily due to the fact that the Central Asian states, while maintaining a modern Muslim identity, are nonetheless oriented in their development towards Western model of economic and forms of government. This gives grounds for the possibility of establishing strategic cooperation between both the regions in the long run. In this regard, the emergence of new states of Central Asia against the background of neighbouring Pakistan and war-torn Afghanistan has been enthusiastically perceived in India (Asanbayev, 2013).

Prime Minister of India, Narendra Modi, visited all the five Central Asian republics in 2015 on way to the Shanghai Cooperation Organization summit in Ufa, Russia. It was a smart strategic and diplomatic step to start trying to overcome difficulties limiting India's role in the region. Although a lot of time has been lost reconnecting with the "land of the Saks", yet, India's interests in the region go far beyond energy and security. These are not only business interests, but civilizational ones, as mentioned above. The visits of Prime Minister Modi to Kazakhstan, Uzbekistan, Tajikistan, Turkmenistan and Kyrgyzstan were symbolic and significant in terms of revitalizing Indian diplomacy in a strategically important region far from India. This visit was also of great importance for expanding the strategic perimeter and perceptions prevailing among our own population about the region outside Pakistan and China.

It is also to be noted that India views Central Asia's political fragility as a source of instability, because the region is on the northern boundary of the Islamic world. Behind the current secular facade is a major shift towards political Islam. The Islamic Movement of Uzbekistan, which has links to Al-Qaeda, continues to have strong positions. Worse, the Islamic State actively recruits supporters in Central Asia. So far, regional regimes are well insured against failing, thanks to Russian support, but the future remains uncertain. The presence of Russia has been the preferred option for India from the very beginning, but its influence in the region is waning. Russia instead seeks to draw closer to China as a result of the sharpening of its own opposition to the West. India is equally concerned about all these issues.

Multi-vector foreign policy of the Central Asian nations,

with the exception of Turkmenistan, has contributed to the establishment of their cooperation with global and regional actors at various levels. In the medium term, India is trying to strengthen its strategic position in Central Asia; however, the direction of Indian foreign policy in Central Asia will be determined by the intersection of mutual interests with major world powers, especially with China, Russia and the United States. In turn, the Central Asian states successfully balance their interaction with external forces through various strategies, ranging from neutrality and multi-vector policies to shifting strategic partners; this allows them to be decisive players in the region.

India views the Shanghai Cooperation Organization members as natural partners in politics and security, as well as in trade and economics. The Shanghai Cooperation Organization brings together all the countries of Central Asia and its neighbours in a single platform, where India, in turn, will be able to interact with all at the same time. India's entry into the Shanghai Cooperation Organization as a full member provides New Delhi with new opportunities to expand its interests in the region (Middle East and Central Asia Analytics, 2017). Today, faced with Russian and Western investment and influence in the region, as well as the rapid growth of China in the regional energy sector, India is having trouble finding its place.

However, there are ample opportunities for cooperation between India and Central Asian countries in the field of traditional and new forms of energy viz. hydrocarbons, hydropower, and resources of the Caspian Sea, nuclear energy, TAPI and CASA1000 projects, as well as technologies for using renewable energy sources (Sayed Masood Sadat, 2015). India's Central Asia policy has gone through the stages of formation, institutionalization and some transformation due to external and internal factors.

Towards Rapprochement between the Regions

In an era of rapid economic growth, energy has become

vital for industrial and technological development of a country. India is one of those countries on whose agenda the task is to expedite rapid economic growth. Geo-economic considerations are an explicit element of India's concerns in its extended neighbourhood concept. There is a sense that South Asia, India's immediate neighbourhood, is too small an economic space for India (Scott, 2009). Of course, India does not have a convincing policy in Central Asia yet. But the visit of Prime Minister Modi gives a clearer outline of this policy. India would like to take part in the process of regional economic integration in Eurasia. But the main problem it faces in Central Asia is the lack of a direct geographical connection.

Access through Iran and Afghanistan or through the North-South international transport corridor is an important goal, but those projects mostly focus on connectivity and pipeline development. Of course, these should not be ruled out, but the delays associated with their implementation are contrary to the economic interests of India. Therefore, to overcome India's geographical isolation from Central Asia and increase its role in the Shanghai Cooperation Organization, Prime Minister Modi has undertaken a number of initiatives that are producing results.

The importance of finding common ground with the regional nations is critical, and the visit of Prime Minister Modi may have given the necessary impetus to improve India's relations with these countries. Modi's active role has been welcome in Central Asia, although India is very late to the table, and will have to make up a lot of ground. From the beginning, Central Asian countries have had high expectations for New Delhi, but India has lagged behind other countries—its trade with the region has only just reached a billion dollars. Many Indian analysts view this visit as an important opportunity to counterbalance China. The presence of the Prime Minister himself seemed to have made a big impression on the people, perhaps no less than what Raj Kapoor, Indira Gandhi and Mithun Chakraborty made.

In addition to bilateral opportunities for cooperation, India has some useful tools to increase its influence in Central Asia. In particular, cooperation within the framework of the Shanghai Cooperation Organization provides India the opportunity to become part of the process of regional cooperation. In this regard, the study of the strategic goals, main directions and priorities of Indian policy in Central Asia, as well as key tools and mechanisms for their implementation in general, are of particular importance.

Within the framework of the joint Intergovernmental Commission on Trade, Economic, Scientific, Technological, Industrial and Cultural Relations, a joint working group on information technology, oil and gas, the textile industry, military-technical cooperation, and international terrorism has been established since the cooperation had come into force. There is also an additional committee on scientific and technical cooperation. Within the framework of the program of technical and economic cooperation with India, young people of Kazakhstan will be trained in the best universities of the country, and our specialists will be able to take advanced training courses. Bilateral ties in the field of culture are being strengthened. Indian filmmakers regularly participate in the international film festival "Eurasia" held in Almaty. Relationships in tourism have also grown in recent years. Since 2006, the Kazakhstan-Indian Fair on Tourism has been held at the Embassy of the Republic of Kazakhstan.

The first meeting of the Ministers of Foreign Affairs of the Republic of Kazakhstan, the Islamic Republic of Afghanistan, the Republic of India, the Kyrgyz Republic, the Republic of Tajikistan, the Republic of Turkmenistan and the Republic of Uzbekistan within the framework of the "India-Central Asia-Afghanistan" Dialogue was held in Samarkand in January 2019. For the purpose of strengthening trade and economic cooperation, the participants stressed the importance of transit potential of the North-South corridor, including the expansion of the Kazakhstan-Turkmenistan-Iran railway route. It is possible to activate the railway connection with the transit-transportation project at the port of Chabahar. This, in turn, will increase the volume of cargo traffic between India and Central Asia, as well as between Russia and Europe.

During the event, issues of economic, cultural and humanitarian cooperation, as well as issues of stabilization and economic development in Afghanistan were discussed. Particularly, issues of intensification of mutual trade, expansion of direct contacts of business associations, development of transit and transport and communication potential of Central Asian countries, promotion of joint initiatives on creation of international and regional transport corridors, attraction of Indian investments, innovations and technologies to Central Asian countries were touched including industry, energy, information technology, pharmaceuticals, agriculture, etc.

Following the meeting, Foreign Ministers of the Dialogue countries adopted a joint statement. The sides noted the dynamic and fruitful development of friendly relations and mutually beneficial cooperation between India and the Central Asian countries and confirmed regional cooperation, mutual support and joint resolution of topical issues for the safe, sustainable and sustainable development of the region.

Conclusion

The Embassy of the Republic of Kazakhstan in India continues its activities aimed at developing and expanding bilateral relations for a mutually beneficial and equal partnership with India, assisting relations in the political, trade, economic, as well as humanitarian fields. In particular, in July 2015, with the active participation of the Embassy, Prime Minister Modi visited Kazakhstan, where important political, trade and economic agreements were reached.

In Kazakhstan, India has not been studied comprehensively. Most attention has been paid to the development of individual areas of cooperation, such as political, economic, energy, but not historical, cultural and humanitarian ties. However, Kazakh-

Indian cooperation in the field of culture has noticeably intensified today. Throughout history, starting from its so-called "Aryan thread" and further the "Silk Road" and the period of the Moguls, there has been a cultural bridge between our regions that mutually enriched and strengthened these ties. The history of relations between our people is full of great men whose actions have served to further their deepening. The brightest of them is Mirzo Muhammad Haydar Dug'lot—an outstanding political figure, commander and scholar of the Middle Ages, equally revered both in Central Asia and in India.

Relations between India and Central Asia, including Kazakhstan, have recently become more active. The population of Central Asia has tremendous liking for Indian culture. In other words, the society here is open to the Indian experience. India, if they wish to help create favourable conditions for the formation of an open society, the introduction and cultivation of democratic values in the countries of Central Asia, would be wise to pay heed to this history.

The renewal of Indian participation in Central Asia indicates that the region is the object of attention of the world's leading players. New Delhi connects the development of relations with the countries of the region with the solution of its issues, which include maintaining peace and stability in the "expanded neighbourhood"; joint coordination of the fight against terrorism and religious extremism; intensification of the fight against drug trafficking; and enhancing energy security and the development of trade and economic relations in the region. Accordingly, by developing regional cooperation with the republics of Central Asia, India seeks to limit the influence of Pakistan, which is viewed by New Delhi as a potential stronghold of international terrorism and Islamic extremism. Despite optimism, many questions remain regarding the prospects for the realization of India's geopolitical interests in Central Asia. After all, as you know, this is not the first attempt by New Delhi to get close to the republics of the region.

Structurally, there is a possibility that India may be over-extending itself with regard to its extended neighbourhood concept. Within this strategic setting, India's easterly and southerly projections into the extended neighbourhood of Southeast Asia and the Indian Ocean have been most substantive, with a degree of pre-eminence being sought in the Indian Ocean for India, as India continues its economics-driven rise. At present, the Indian government has set a goal to actively pursue its interests in Central Asia.

References

"A National Security Strategy for a New Washington, D.C.: The White House", May 1997, available at: http://history.defense.gov/resources/nss1997.pdf.

"Analytical Portal, "Humanitarian Technologies": Rating of Countries of the World in Terms of GDP", 2018, available at: https://gtmarket.ru/ratings/rating-countries-gdp/rating-countries-gdp-info.

Asanbayev, M., Online Portal: Kazakhstan Centre of Humanitarian and Political Trends, "India's Policy in Central Asia", 2013, available at: http://www.sarap.kz/index.php/ru/rubikon/212-politika-indii-v-tsentralnoj-azii.html.

Analytical Portal, "Middle East and Central Asia Analytics", "India in the SCO", 2017, available at: http://kazanalytics.kz/индия-в-шос-перспективы-и-вызовы.

"India Population (2019)": Worldometers, available at: https://www.worldometers.info/world-population/india-population.

Kazantsev, A., "Five Scenarios for the Future Borders of Central Asia", available at: https://russiancouncil.ru/en/analytics-and-comments/analytics/five-scenarios-for-the-future-borders-of-central-asia.

Kydyrbekuly, D. (2003), "Geostrategy of US in Kazakhstan: From Global to Small Dimension", Almaty, Kazakhstan, p. 280.

Kumar, V. Sanil, Pathak, K.C., Pednekar, P. and Raju, N.S.N. (2006), "Coastal Processes along the Indian Coastline", *Current Science,* 91(4): 530-536.

Maksudov, A. (2018), "The Current Central Asia as a Geographical-

Political Concept is an Invention of the Post-Soviet Period", 2018, "Zonakz.net", available at: https://zonakz.net/2018/12/20/nyneshnyaya-centralnaya-aziya-kak-geograficheskо-politicheskoe-ponyatie-eto-izobretenie-postsovetskogo-perioda.

Mukherjee, Pranab (2006), "Indian Foreign Policy: A Road Map for the Decade Ahead", available at: https://www.mea.gov.in/Speeches-Statements.htm?dtl/2395.

Raina, R. (2010), "Echoes of a Distant Past: India and Kazakhstan", New Delhi.

Sadat, Sayed Masood (2015), "TAPI and CASA-1000: Win-win Trade between Central Asia and South Asia", Norwegian Institute of International Affairs, OSCE Academy.

Shabalin A. (2018), "Middle and Central Asia: Are There any Differences between Them?", "Kaktotak", available at: https://kaktakto.com/poznavatelno/centralnaya-i-srednyaya-aziya-est-li-mezhdu-nimi-razlichiya.

8

Conclusion

Kashif Hasan Khan

Towards the end of 20th century, new states showed up on the political map of the world, which were earlier part of the previous Soviet Union. After the breakdown of the Soviet system, CARs picked up autonomy, which made it conceivable to set up free ties for participation with all nations of the world. This circumstance excited incredible enthusiasm among created and extraordinary nations, for example, China, USA, Russia, Turkey and India. These nations ended up dynamic so as to have solid accomplices in the area of Central Asia. India, in this procedure as one of the significant nations of South Asia, started to lead conciliatory relations with the point of re-establishing and fortifying ties between the two states and the people of the nations.

In the Soviet years, the Indian nearness in the locale was acknowledged through Moscow. Indian movies, music, and move have involved a unique spot among the inclinations of Uzbeks, Tajiks, Kazakhs and different people groups of the locale. As a monetary accomplice, India was basically seen as a producer and provider of value drugs. These variables, thus, added to the useful and reliable advancement of connection between the two regions. Moreover, India has always been as a nation with a rich history and interesting society, which the CAR individuals have shared for all intents and purpose for a considerable length of time. Notwithstanding, during the Soviet period, India had hotter relations with Central Asia.

In 1991, the breakdown of the USSR irritated India. The purpose behind this uneasiness was the likelihood of the development of an Islamic coalition in the Central Asian

Republics, which slanted towards religiously extreme powers. This could have negatively affected the further improvement of relations and interests in the nations of the locale. Geopolitical interests and vitality wellsprings of the district was critical to India for the improvement of dynamism.

India had strong establishments for building up collaboration in every aspect of life. They connected each other by authentic and social qualities, normal conventions, which caused it conceivable to further develop bilateral social and compassionate collaboration. The historical backdrop of relations among India and Central Asia, specifically, Uzbekistan, was established in days of yore. Chronicled certainties and unearthings concerning the Kushan kingdom demonstrate the suppositions. Simply take a gander at a portion of the Indian see sights to see how solid and cosy connections have connected the people of Central Asia.

Uzbekistan, in fact, was the first country in the region to establish official contacts with India before the collapse of the USSR. India is one of those countries that recognized the independence of the Republic of Uzbekistan (December 26, 1991). On March 18, 1992, the Protocol on the Establishment of Diplomatic Relations was signed in Tashkent. In September 1992, the consulate of Uzbekistan was opened in New Delhi, which was transformed in 1994 to the embassy of the Republic of Uzbekistan. On August 1988 (during the Soviet times), the Consulate General of India was established in Tashkent, which was transformed in 1992 to an embassy.

In March 1992, embassy of India was opened in Tashkent and a pact was signed on the establishment of diplomatic relations at the embassy level between the two countries. This in turn testifies Uzbekistan and India as two independent states of the world community, observing legal international norms for a mutually beneficial, equal basis, free all-round cooperation. Gaining independence led to an opportunity to strengthen cooperation and bring the countries and their people closer. During the time of the former Soviet Union, President of Uzbekistan Islam Karimov visited India on August 17-19, 1991.

In that event, the first steps were put on a new stage of interstate relations. This was the period of the first official visit to India of the leader from the Republic of Uzbekistan, and this was an expression of the formation of a new stage in the foreign policy of Uzbekistan. As a result of this visit, President Karimov expressed hope that the meeting between the leaders of the two countries and between representatives of public and business circles would provide an impetus for the establishment of qualitatively new relations between Uzbekistan and India.

In May 1993, the Prime Minister of the Republic of India, Narasimha Rao, made a significant contribution to the strengthening and expansion of Uzbek-Indian relations in a qualitatively new stage of international relations. During this visit, documents were signed that were of great importance for further cooperation of the states. The agreement "On intergovernmental relations and cooperation between the Republic of Uzbekistan and the Republic of India" was signed expressing the desire to develop an all-round and mutually beneficial cooperation between Uzbekistan and India. Tashkent and New Delhi have always been ready to cooperate in the framework of their interests in all spheres of the society. The visits of officials in 2018 from both the sides shows that in future, diplomatic relations will continue to develop and this will help strengthen further cooperation. The last visit of the President of the Republic of Uzbekistan to India would surely contribute to the achievement of common goals while raising cooperation between the two countries to a qualitatively new level.

In the early years of independence, CARs needed a reliable partner in South Asia on diplomatic front. However, due to internal socio-economic factors at that time, India could not pay enough attention while designing foreign policy for Central Asia. In spite of this, the prosperous geographical position and large raw material and energy resources of this region has always attracted India. Diplomatic ties between the two regions have acquired a completely new meaning, corresponding to modern international cooperation requirements. It should be noted that since the period of independence, the ongoing transformations have aroused great interest among leaders, politicians and journalists of India.

The historical backdrop of participation among Kyrgyzstan and India likewise starts with the Great Silk Road. What's more, obviously, it was political, yet in addition, it was also financial and social participation with the previous USSR. After the surprising visit of Indira Gandhi, and later on of Rajiv Gandhi, numerous babies started to be called by Indian names. The young ladies were called Indira, and the young men Rajiv. This is one of the splendid images of a well-disposed signal towards the Asian state. An entire age of Soviet Kyrgyz individuals, and natives of our nation, yet in addition numerous Asian republics, recall Indian movies being great and shrewd, about affection and filled with incredible delight. Practically, every show of the Indian movies was held in inaccessible towns with a full house and jam-packed lobbies of clubs.

Not understanding the substance of the words, however remembering the expressions of their main tunes, older individuals sang Indian tunes at stylized occasions and festivities. With autonomy, Kyrgyzstan started to construct its discretionary relations with different nations. Today, there are numerous natives in the nation who have gotten instructions in India, have finished PG courses, have studied the English language, and so forth. The program of the First President of the nation A. Akaev, "Work force of the 21st Century", made remarkable achievements.

It should be emphasized that inter-parliamentary contacts have also been maintained between the two regions. Political consultations are regularly held within the framework of interaction among the foreign affairs agencies. The last round of political consultations took place in March 2019 in New

Delhi, where a detailed analysis was made of the state of bilateral relations in political, trade, economic, cultural, and humanitarian and other fields, as well as in the field of cooperation within the UN, SCO and other international organizations. Such inter-governmental meetings contribute to the convergence of positions on political and security issues at a regional and global level, the expansion of trade, the implementation of joint mutually beneficial production projects, including the free economic zones.

India is not mentioned in any of the Central Asia countries' strategy papers, nor does India name any of the Central Asian countries in its own strategy paper. However, both have signed several agreements. Recently, India and Kazakhstan have signed agreements including memoranda of understanding on defence cooperation, as well as transportation and transit (e.g. the multilateral, multimodal 'Ashgabat Agreement', which seeks to create a transport and transit corridor between India, Iran, Kazakhstan, Oman, Turkmenistan and Uzbekistan).

India and Tajikistan have concluded agreements on cooperation in countering terrorism and terror financing, money laundering, intelligence sharing, joint military training, and defence cooperation. India and Uzbekistan have signed agreements covering cultural cooperation and tourism, trade and investment, and transportation and transit. India and Kyrgyzstan have signed agreements on defence cooperation, tourism, agriculture, and youth affairs. India and Turkmenistan have signed agreements on defence cooperation and transit and transportation.

It ought to be accentuated that in India, the quality of education and training has been improving. The most prevalent claim to fame in the colleges of India includes data innovation and pharmacology. Towards the start of 2019, Amity University from India established its campus in Tashkent and later on arranged for building up another university in Bishkek, Kyrgyzstan.

By and large, further fortifying of reciprocal relations among India and CARs meets the long-haul interests of the nations and has opened doors for an increasingly successful collaboration within the political, economic, and social circles.

Bibliography and Web Links

Bibliography and Web Links

Alden, C. and Aran, A. (2017), "Foreign Policy Analysis: New Approaches", London and New York: Routledge.

Anceschi, Luca (2015), "Turkmenistan's Export Crisis: Is TAPI the Answer?", Central Asia Policy Brief 27, available at: http://centralasiaprogram.org/wp-content/uploads/2015/06/Policy-Brief-27-June-2015.pdf.

Asian Development Bank Institute (2016), "Connecting Central Asia with Economic Centres", Brookings Institution Press.

Balooch, Mahmoud (2009), "Iran and India's Cooperation in Central Asia", *China and Eurasia Forum Quarterly*, Vol. 7, No. 3 pp. 25-29.

Baumer, C. (2012), "The History of Central Asia: The Age of the Steppe Warriors", New York: I.B. Tauris & Co. Ltd.

Bhattacherjee, K. (2017), "India Ships Wheat to Afghanistan via Chabahar", *The Hindu*, New Delhi.

Blanchard, Jean-Marc F. and Flint, Colin (2017), "The Geopolitics of China's Maritime Silk Road Initiative", *Geopolitics*, Vol. 22, No. 2, pp. 223-245.

Blank, S. (2007), "U.S. Interests in Central Asia and Their Challenges", *Demokratizatsiya*, 15(3).

Brauer, B. (2012), "Foreign Direct Investors and National Politics", in A. Heinrich and H. Pleines (eds.), 'Challenges of the Caspian Resource Boom: Domestic Elites and Policy-Making', London: Palgrave Macmillan.

Breuning, M. (2007), "Foreign Policy Analysis: A Comparative Introduction", New York: Palgrave Macmillan.

Bunce, V. (1999), "The Political Economy of Post-socialism", *Slavic Review*, 58(4), pp. 756-793.

Chandra, Amiya (2015), "India-Central Asia Relations: The Economic Dimension", New Delhi: Pentagon Press.

Chandra, S. (2007), "History of Medieval India", Hyderabad: Orient Longman Private Ltd.

Chaudhuri, B. and Sethi, M. (2010), "India-China Interactions in Central Asia through the Prism of Paul Kennedy's Analysis of Great Powers", in M. Laruelle, J.F. Huchet, S. Peyrouse and B. Balci (eds.), 'China and India in Central Asia: A New Great

Game?', New York: Palgrave Macmillan.

Cox, R. (1987), "Production, Power, and World Order: Social Forces in the Making of History", New York: Columbia University Press.

Dani, Ahmad Hassan (1996), "Central Asia Today", Lahore: Sang-e-Meel Publication.

Djaka, A. (2005), "South Asia and Central Asia: Geopolitical Dynamics", Jaipur: Mangal Deep Publications.

Foltz, R.C. (1998), "Mughal India and Central Asia", New Delhi: Oxford University Press.

Gopal, Surender (2005), "Understanding Central Asia and India: The Soviet and Post-Soviet Era", New Delhi: Shipra Publications.

Gulshan, S. (2010), "Regional Economic Linkages", in N. Joshi (ed.), 'Reconnecting India and Central Asia: Emerging Security and Economic Dimensions', New Delhi: Pentagon Press.

Hiro, Dilip (2010), "Inside Central Asia", India, Noida: Harper Collins.

Hudson, V.M. (2014), "Foreign Policy Analysis: Classic and Contemporary Theory", Lanham, USA: Rowman & Littlefield.

Kabir, S. and Salim, R.A. (2011), "Parallel Integration and ASEAN-EU Trade Potential: An Empirical Analysis", *Journal of Economic Integration*, Vol. 26, No. 4, December, pp. 601-623.

Kapur, A. (2006), "India: From Regional to World Power", London and New York: Routledge.

Kassab, H.S. (2018), "Grand Strategies of Weak States and Great Powers", Cham, Switzerland: Palgrave Macmillan.

Khan, Nasir Raza (2016), "Indian and Central Asia: Geopolitics, Economics and Culture", New Delhi: Primus Books.

Laruelle, M. and Peyrouse, S. (eds.) (2011), "Mapping Central Asia: Indian Perceptions and Strategies", Ashgate.

Laruelle, M. (2008), "Rusian Eurasianism: An Ideology of Empire", Baltimore: The Johns Hopkins University Press.

Laumullin, M. (2006), "The Contemporary Geopolitical Situation in Central Asia and India's Interests", in K. Santhanam and B.K. Sultanov (eds.), 'India-Kazakhstan Relations: Enhancing the Partnership', New Delhi: Anamaya Publishers.

Malik, I.A. (2014), "India's Trade Potential with Central Asia: An Application of Gravity Model Analysis", *International Journal on World Peace*, 7(3).

Marer, Paul (1985), "Dollar GNPs of the U.S.S.R. and Eastern

Europe", Baltimore, MD: Johns Hopkins University Press.

McNabb, D.E. (2016), "Vladimir Putin and Russia's Imperial Revival", London and New York: CRC Press.

Morton, A. (2007), "Unravelling Gramsci: Hegemony and Passive Revolution in the Global Political Economy", London: Pluto Press.

Pannier, B. (2015), "The Trans-Caspian Pipeline: Technically Possible, Politically Difficult", Radio Free Europe/Radio Liberty, available at: http://www.rferl.org/a/turkmenistan-natural-gas-europe-pipeline-tcp/27033746.html.

Peyrouse, S. (2007), "Economic Aspects of Chinese-Central Asia Rapprochement", Silk Road Paper, Uppsala University.

"Russia Backs India's Case for SCO Membership", *The Times of India*, June 12, 2010.

Starr, S. Frederick (ed.) (2007), "The New Silk Roads: Transport and Trade in Greater Central Asia", Washington D.C.: Central Asia-Caucasus Institute, p. 31.

Svante, Cornell and Regine Spector (2002), "Central Asia More than Islamic Extremists", *The Washington Quarterly*, Winter.

Thapar, Romila (2000), "A History of India", Vol. 1, 12th edition, New Delhi: Penguin Books.

The World Economic Forum Report (2016), "Jobs, Jobs, Jobs", presentation by secretary general, World Tourism Organisation, available at: http://reports.weforum.org/travel-and-tourism-competitiveness-report-2017/tourism-and-job-creation-advancing-the-2030-development-agenda.

Umarov, P. (ed.), "Tajikistan in the 21st Century: Society, Politics and Economy", New Delhi: Pentagon Press.

United Nations Office on Drugs and Crime (2007), "Securing Central Asia's Borders with Afghanistan", September.

World Population Review (2019), "Total Population by Country 2019", available at: http://worldpopulationreview.com/countries.

Zhukov, S. (2009), "Uzbekistan: A Domestically Oriented Gas Producer", in S. Pirani (ed.), 'Russian and CIS Gas Markets and Their Impact on Europe', Oxford: Oxford University Press.

Important Web Links on Central Asia

http://www.cacianalyst.org/
https://eurasianet.org/
http://www.silk-road.com/
https://iwpr.net/
http://www.eaeunion.org/?lang=en
http://www.osce-academy.net/en/research/researchpapers/
https://www.csis.org/
http://www.asianamerican.net/centralasia.html
https://escas-cess.auca.kg/
https://www.carecprogram.org/
https://www.usaid.gov/central-asia-regional
https://www.uzbekistan.org/
https://voicesoncentralasia.org/
https://ec.europa.eu/trade/policy/countries-and-regions/regions/central-asia/
https://www.unodc.org/centralasia/
https://www.icef.com/events/icef-central-asia-focus/
https://www.crisisgroup.org/europe-central-asia/central-asia/central-asia-decay-and-decline
https://creeca.wisc.edu/

Index

Index